361.70681
40P

South Asian Funding in the U

GW00645171

WALTHAM FOREST

PUBLIC LIBRARIES

Kari

with Z

REFERENCE LIBRARY

DIRECTORY OF SOCIAL CHANGE

WITHDRAWN

FOR SALE

WALTHAM FOREST LIBRARIES

023 169 312

Published by:
The Directory of Social Change
24 Stephenson Way
London NW1 2DP
Tel: 0171 209 5151 (020 7209 5151), Fax: 0171 209 5049 (020 7209 5049)
e-mail: info@dsc.org.uk
website: http://www.dsc.org.uk
from whom further copies and a full publications list are available.

The Directory of Social Change is a Registered Charity no. 800517

© The Directory of Social Change 1999

All rights reserved. **No part of this book may be stored in a retrieval system or reproduced in any form whatsoever without the prior permission in writing of the publisher.** This book is sold subject to the condition that it shall not, by way of trade or otherwise, be lent, re-sold, hired out or otherwise circulated without the publisher's prior permission in any form of binding or cover other than that in which it is published and without a similar condition being imposed on the subsequent purchaser.

ISBN 1 900360 16 0

British Library Cataloguing in Publication Data
A catalogue record of this book is available from the British Library

Cover design by Kate Bass
Typeset by David McLean
Printed and bound by Antony Rowe, Chippenham

Directory of Social Change London office:
Courses and conferences tel: 0171 209 4949 (020 7209 4949)
Charityfair tel: 0171 209 1015 (020 7209 1015)
Research tel: 0171 209 4422 (020 7209 4422)
Finance and Administration tel: 0171 209 0902 (020 7209 0902)

Directory of Social Change Liverpool office
3rd floor, Federation House, Hope Street, Liverpool L1 9BW
Research tel: 0151 708 0136
Courses and conferences tel: 0151 708 0117

Contents

WALTHAM FOREST PUBLIC LIBRARIES	
02316931	
CYP	24.01.01
	£9.95
NR	

Acknowledgements

I would like to thank the numerous people who have been involved in the various stages of the development of this report, particularly Paul Caddick, Mark Lattimer, Anne Mountfield, Michael Norton and Anthony Wilson. Grateful thanks also to all those who agreed to be interviewed, including Sarwar Ahmed, Arif Ali, Mohammed Akbar Ali, Ramola Bachchan, Kamlesh Bahl, Gopal Bhanot, Ashvinkumar Bosamin, Harpal Brar, Nasser Butt, Lena Choudary, Rusi Dalal, Akhandadhi Das, Navnit Doholakia, Thrity Engineer, Ram Gidoomal, Jane Grant, Sister Jayanti, Hoshang Jungalwalla, Kristine Landon-Smith, Rabi Martins, Nancy Mitchell, Narendhra Morar, Tara Mukherjee, Kanti Nagda, Ruxana Noon, Kate Parminter, Tara Parveen, Indira Patel, Vanita Patel, Usha Prashar, Vikram Shah, Shiv Sharma, Anil Tandon, Farrokh Vajifdar and Iqbal Wahhab.

Thanks are also due both to the Confederation of Indian Organisations for kindly allowing access to their research and to the many trust secretaries, trustees and trust volunteers who provided information for the funding section of this report.

Additional thanks are due to the Hilden Charitable Fund and the Joseph Rowntree Charitable Trust for providing some funding towards this project and the Directory of Social Change's publications department for their patience!

Lastly I owe special thanks to Zerbanoo Gifford who has been involved throughout the development of this report, for her humour, patience and her belief in a better future for Britain's black and minority community voluntary sector. Zerbanoo is a campaigner and writer. Her books include *Dadabhai Naoroji, Britain's First Asian MP*; *Asian Presence in Europe*; *The Golden Thread*; and *Thomas Clarkson and the Campaign Against Slavery*.

The Directory of Social Change is an independent voice for positive social change, set up in 1975 to help voluntary and community organisations become more effective. We do this by providing practical, challenging and affordable information and training to meet the current, emerging and future needs of the sector.

Karina Holly was until 1999 the editor of *Trust Monitor*, published by the Directory of Social Change.

The research for *South Asian Funding in the UK* was supported by grant funding from the **Joseph Rowntree Charitable Trust** and the **Hilden Charitable Fund**.

Preface

■■■■■■■■■■■■■■■■■■■■■■■■■■■■■■■■■■■■■■

This report appears (summer 1999) at a time when the profile of South Asian people in the UK has never been higher. 1997 marked 50 years since Indian independence and the partition and birth of Pakistan, 26 years since the formation of Bangladesh, as well as the 25th anniversary of Idi Amin's expulsion of Asians from Uganda. In the final years of the twentieth century, the financial and political might of Britain's South Asian population has come to the fore. However, whilst wealthy UK South Asians are now actively courted by politicians and fundraisers alike there is still a dearth of information about their input into the fabric of modern British society. Stereotypes of isolated and insular communities continue to predominate throughout the media, which consistently fails to present a balanced view of the multicultural reality that is British society.

South Asian Funding in the UK aims to give an insight into the role South Asian people in the UK are playing in shaping the way charity is taken forward into the next millennium. The research for this book was carried out between 1996 and 1999 and included a number of interviews with prominent players within the various South Asian communities now actively present in Britain. These interviews present the personal perspectives of individual South Asians in Britain today and in no way should be considered representative of the UK's South Asian communities as a whole.

WALTHAM FOREST PUBLIC LIBRARIES

The purpose of the report

The impetus for the report came from a growing dissatisfaction with the available statistical information on the UK voluntary sector, which all too often neglects to acknowledge the input, needs and values of minority ethnic community groups. Coupled with the knowledge that the voluntary sector in the UK represents a far broader social and cultural spectrum than hitherto acknowledged, it was also felt that a whole new set of funders had emerged unrecognised. There are many thousands of small voluntary and community organisations serving Britain's South Asian and other minority ethnic communities and whilst they are actively seeking charitable funding, it is not one-way traffic. South Asians are contributing substantially to the growth of the UK's voluntary sector. Although information is still scarce, *South Asian Funding in the UK* includes the first listing of trusts set up by or for UK South Asians.

How the report is structured

The report is in two sections.

Section One covers the background to the growth of Britain's South Asian communities, some basic facts and figures, the funding crisis facing Britain's South Asian voluntary sector as well as the potential for optimism about future funding. It examines:

- the nature of South Asian communities in the UK
- funding needs of minority ethnic community groups
- funding opportunities
- representation and the voluntary sector
- eradicating colour-blind funding
- the way forward

Section Two includes a listing of grant-making trusts with connections to the South Asian voluntary sector.

NOTE: The abbreviated references given in brackets refer to sources listed in the Bibliography at the end of the book.

Introduction

It is not easy to present a coherent analysis of the role played by South Asians in the UK's constantly evolving voluntary sector and invariably the result is full of contradictions. Clearly it is difficult to isolate any so-called 'South Asian' community, either from within the dominant British culture or from the multitude of cultures which exist in South Asia. As a recent report by the Confederation of Indian Organisations notes: 'the Council for Sikh Gurudwaras felt that Sikh people did not want to be labelled as "Indian",' whilst 'a Hindu organisation also felt that the term "Asian" often obscures their individual needs and takes resources away from them.'

Rozina Visram argues in *Peopling of London*, 'Asians in Britain have different national, regional, urban and rural origins, with different traditions and expectations'. In contrast to Asian immigrants, South Asians born in Britain are likely to have a whole new set of perceptions which lead to slightly different expectations. In the face of this it might be considered foolhardy to attempt an analysis of South Asian philanthropy in the UK.

Despite these reservations, this report was undertaken in order to demonstrate the cultural vibrancy of the UK voluntary sector, in which all the members of Britain's majority and minority communities have an equal stake. However, we fully accept that this report is limited in its scope and may sometimes use the very stereotypes and generalisations it is attempting to refute.

'South Asians' are often referred to collectively in this way, a generalisation based on assumptions which largely exclude the range of cultures, languages, religions and traditions which the label should be understood to include. However, despite this, for the purposes of this research the term has proved useful as a means of distinguishing South Asian communities both from other minority communities in the UK and from the mainstream white culture.

Much has been made of the growing economic position of the UK's South Asian population. Indeed the stereotype of the Asian corner shopkeeper working long hours and meanwhile amassing a substantial fortune is one now firmly embedded in British culture. Throughout the last decade, the growing economic muscle of UK South Asians has meant there has at last been a concerted effort to court their influence by the major political parties. When John

Major welcomed leading Asian businessmen into Number 10 on the first anniversary of his succession, he publicly ushered in a new group of seriously wealthy entrepreneurs worthy of political interest. Tony Blair has been keen to continue the courtship.

The South Asian voluntary sector, whilst not a cohesive or united grouping, is part of a black voluntary sector which is at the forefront of community-based work. Identifying needs, developing a range of services tailored to meet these needs, and finding significant levels of funding from within Britain's South Asian communities, it is a sector which is fiercely independent, if by necessity. It is also a sector which has its roots in a variety of cultures which have traditionally relied on the support of the family. The South Asian voluntary sector has in part arisen out of a need to replicate the services hitherto provided by families within communities and which, for a variety of reasons, are not being provided by the state.

South Asian Funding in the UK provides a snapshot of how the voluntary sector in the UK today is a vibrant, constantly evolving and multicultural entity. In doing so, it hopes to prompt funders, policy makers and charities themselves to address the questions which are being asked within both the South Asian and other minority ethnic communities about why minority ethnic community organisations are often last in the queue for charitable funding.

Efforts to encourage members of Britain's South Asian communities to get involved in mainstream politics in Britain have hitherto to a large extent been disappointing, probably because they have failed to address the needs of disadvantaged Asian communities, instead placing an undue emphasis on courting wealthy individuals.

Funders of specifically South Asian voluntary organisations are undoubtedly scarce. The lack of a distinct funding pool for the minority ethnic communities which fall under this umbrella contrasts strongly with the resources available to Jewish community groups, which have clear sources of financial support available, not least in the many hundreds of grant-making trusts which prioritise giving to Jewish causes. There are many reasons for this, not least an understandable reluctance by South Asians in the UK to be perceived as a single community. In a report for the Institute of Jewish Policy Research, Margaret Harris refers to the cohesive nature of the Jewish voluntary sector. In contrast to the position frequently adopted by South Asians, she notes that: 'Jews in the UK often refer to themselves collectively as the Jewish community'.

However, in the South Asian voluntary sector, the divisions between South Asian communities can be as deep as those between South Asians and the mainstream white culture. The Jewish voluntary sector also has the financial advantage of a far longer commercial history in the UK, dating back at least to the eighteenth century.

The debate on the future of the South Asian voluntary sector is not one of minority interest. Many of the issues are relevant to a mainstream audience as they concern the future of the voluntary sector as a whole: the struggle for survival, securing resources, ensuring accountability and meeting a broad range of needs. Furthermore, the UK voluntary sector's 'colour-blind' approach to the various needs of minority ethnic community organisations demands an urgent reassessment. Following the recent Macpherson Report on the Stephen Lawrence Inquiry and the official recognition of the endemic institutionalised racism within the Metropolitan Police, there is likely to be a big shake-up. One of Macpherson's central recommendations is to extend the powers of the Commission of Racial Equality to cover all organs of state. The Institute for Public Policy Research is spearheading a campaign for the creation of a 'one-stop shop' massively extending anti-discrimination law to make it 'unlawful for any public body to discriminate against anyone on racial grounds'. That this is not already law only serves to underline the uphill struggle facing not only the South Asian and minority ethnic voluntary sector, but also every individual from an ethnic minority community living in Britain today.

'... the success of Asian incomers will make Britain in 1999 resemble [multicultural] California' (*The Economist*)

In its third 'rich list' of Asians in Britain, *Eastern Eye* notes, '*The Economist* claimed that Asian families (especially those from East Africa) will be better off than the average white in the year ahead. The proportion of Asians attending UK universities will be higher than that of indigenous whites; and they will, on average, achieve higher grades. The typical British economist and business school graduate will soon be Asian'. First and second generation Asians have made their impact, but in the next millennium it is the third and fourth generation Asians who will make the biggest impact. Already their commercial success is noticeable. It is only a matter of time before this educational and economic success spawns a goldmine of charitable funding. The key question for the next millennium is where this charitable funding will go. In the years to come their philanthropic might will undoubtedly be felt.

Section One

■ ■

How a new voluntary sector came into being

Britain's wealthiest and Britain's poorest

The ethnic make-up of modern Britain is more diverse than ever before. South Asians number 1.5 million, representing 3 per cent of the population as a whole. They now constitute the largest single minority community in Britain and are also its richest, with a total wealth put by some at £5 billion. It is however a community of extremes, ranging from billionaire entrepreneurs such as Lakshmi Mittal (who according to *The Sunday Times* has a fortune of £2 billion and is the UK's third wealthiest individual) and the hugely successful Hinduja family, to some of the most disadvantaged and discriminated against people in the country.

It is also a community that is now being courted by various political parties. From John Major's inaugural anniversary dinner as Prime Minister in 1991 to Tony Blair's soundings, in his first party conference speech as Prime Minister, on the need to broaden politics' appeal to minority communities there have been clear albeit woefully overdue signs that South Asians now have both political and financial muscle. Throwing aside stereotypes of impoverished communities, British South Asians are now referred to in glowing terms as the '£5 billion opportunity' and as a 'profitable market for non-profits'. Such superlatives have at last meant that the mainstream voluntary sector is now looking towards Britain's South Asian communities. However, the potential revenue may prove elusive, as the vast majority of voluntary organisations do not work directly within South Asian communities and are dependent almost exclusively on white support. This situation is likely to remain unchanged so long as their client base and the staff and volunteers remain predominantly white. As a result there are justified claims within South Asian communities that their needs are not being met by the mainstream voluntary sector and that South Asian voluntary organisations offer unique rather than replicated services. Arguing that mainstream voluntary organisations have either consciously or unconsciously excluded black communities from their remits for long periods of time, a Telethon report has noted the important role played by black and other minority ethnic voluntary organisations: 'It is now proving difficult for such [mainstream voluntary] organisations to adapt their policies and practice sufficiently to gain access to Black networks and to offer appropriate and effective provision ... All of this has added to the ability of Black voluntary groups to offer services which are qualitatively different to those offered by the white voluntary sector' (*Black Perspectives in the Voluntary Sector*, 1993).

We are here because you were there

More than fifty years after the partition of India in 1947 and twenty-five years after the first influx of East African Asians following Idi Amin's expulsion of Ugandan Asians, Britain is continuing to reap the benefits of its colonial past. However the bounty has changed. The last decade has seen an explosion in the numbers of charitable trusts being set up by wealthy and community-minded individuals from Britain's South Asian communities keen to invest in the country's social fabric.

Despite the acute financial need of many voluntary organisations working within Britain's South Asian and other minority ethnic communities, these new Asian grant-making trusts do not appear to be particularly striving to pioneer giving within their own communities (see Section Two). Whilst some trusts clearly target need within their own communities, others appear more interested in conforming to a less selfless model of philanthropy – gestural giving. In a recent lecture the secretary of the Joseph Rowntree Charitable Trust criticised donors in this interpretation of philanthropy stating, 'The very nature of much giving – indeed probably most giving – is such as to comfort the powerful, either directly through paying for their pleasures (art galleries and opera houses) or through doing good to the poor and dispossessed in such ways as only serve to keep them in that position'. (Steven Burkeman, 1999 Allen Lane Lecture). Whilst it is obviously not only trusts set up by Asians which might slot into this category, it is not surprising that many South Asian community organisations feel let down by the wealthier members of their communities. Kusum Joshi, Information Officer for the Confederation of Indian Organisations, is less than overwhelmed by the level of grants made to the South Asian voluntary sector from either within or outside the UK's South Asian communities. Wealthy South Asians in Britain do not appear to be responding in large numbers to calls from grassroots groups. 'Very often, wealthy individuals want to support high profile causes', she explained, 'and do not appear to be aware of the needs of community organisations'.

High profile donations by South Asians, most notably the £1 million given to London Zoo by Lord Paul's foundation, whilst having a clear impact, have also attracted criticism, prompting leading Asian businessman, Gulam

Noon, to call for an awakening amongst Britain's South Asians. 'Swraj Paul giving £1 million to London Zoo is fantastic', Noon conceded, 'but at the same time we need to look at our own charities. We need to make sure that we are recognised.'

Origins of South Asian communities in the UK

Everyone who lives in Britain today is an immigrant or the descendant of an immigrant. However, Britain has done much to deny its multicultural past and many people remain unaware of the immense contribution made by immigrants from many nations. In an effort to rectify this, in 1996 the Commission for Racial Equality launched its *Roots for the Future* project, which celebrated Britain's long history of ethnic diversity. Prior to the major influxes of South Asians, there were many ways in which Britain had gained from its colonial ties. In 1914 more than 1.5 million Indians enlisted for the British armed forces, with at least 40,000 killed in the ensuing war. In what became the largest volunteer force in history, 2.5 million Indians fought in the British armed forces during the Second World War.

Charity goes West

Charity is not peculiar to the West. Nor apparently is the post-colonial tokenism of helping poorer nations. Sir Jamsetji Jeejeebhoy became one of the nineteenth century's richest businessmen, despite inauspicious origins washing bottles in his uncle's factory in India as an orphaned teenager. He subsequently gave away around two thirds of his vast fortune to good causes around the world. When Ireland faced famine in 1822 and 1846 and severe floods hit France in 1856, he sent substantial sums of money to both countries. The Jamsetji Jeejeebhoy Parsi Benevolent Institution continues working in his name today, together with the other bodies he founded, including the first general and obstetric hospitals in Bombay, as well as the country's first art school. He was knighted by the British in 1822, given the Freedom of the City of London in 1855 and became the first Asian Baronet in 1857.

Contrary to popular myth there has been a strong South Asian presence in Britain since at least the seventeenth century, following the establishment of the East India Company in 1600 (*Peopling of London,* 1993). In Scotland there is even said to have been a 'considerable number' of Indians settled as early as 1540. By the eighteenth century the Indian immigrant population of wealthy princes and employees of the East India Company had expanded to include Ayahs, the Indian domestic servants who had become fashionable amongst the white elite, in addition to a growing number of students and performance artists. From the mid-nineteenth century large numbers of Asian professionals began to arrive in Britain; lawyers, doctors, academics and students, retired civil servants, merchants and traders.

However, there was no steady flow of immigrants from the sub-continent until the First World War, when many Indians were recruited as seamen for the Royal Navy and Merchant Navy. Many of them subsequently settled in Britain and from then on there were successive waves of South Asian immigrants. In the 1920s, there was an influx of mainly single male Sikhs, who arrived from the Punjab looking for work and stayed for several years at a time. One of the earliest Indian restaurants in Britain was established in Leicester Square in 1920, although, in fact, 'curry' had been added to the menu of the Norris Street Coffee House as far back as 1773.

It was in the 1950s and 1960s that large-scale settlement of Indians and Pakistanis, the largest South Asian communities in Britain, really began to take off, and with it the spread of the Indian curry house. The post-war reconstruction of Britain and the booming economy meant there was an acute labour shortage in Britain. This coincided with the upheaval following the partition of India in 1947. Ex-non-commissioned army officers, doctors and teachers were followed by those with rural backgrounds largely from the Punjab, Gujarat, Sylhet and Kashmir who settled in the areas of rapid industrial growth. The rate of influx was intense. In 1951 there were 350 Asians resident in Southall in London. By the mid-1960s, Asians constituted 12 per cent of the Southall population.

The differing experience of the respective Asian communities in Britain cannot be over-emphasised. A reflection of this diversity is the huge range of voluntary sector groups that have developed, representing different community needs, and demonstrating the cultural, religious, economic and social needs of each community, as well as the relative wealth of each group.

The 'ethnic question'

In Britain, the official census ethnic origin categories have long been the subject of debate, accused primarily of over-simplifying ethnic diversity (*1991 Census*, 1996). The *1991 Census of Great Britain* asked a question on ethnicity for the first time, but met with intense opposition. Arguments that as in principle all citizens are equal before the law any questions relating to socially constructed identities heighten divisions were countered by the argument that inequality along ethnic lines can only be corrected once it is quantified.

In reality the 'ethnic question' on the census probably does not reveal the true size of Britain's minority communities. Although it attempted to rid the census of past controversies encountered through basing ethnicity on country of birth, it was not without controversy itself. The Islamic Secretariat of the UK campaigned for Muslims not to answer the ethnic group question and to put 'Muslim' on the form instead (Islamic Secretariat, 1991). Whilst country of birth is unambiguous, albeit with built-in anomalies (the 1991 census revealed that 15 per cent of people living in Britain but born in India are white), ethnic identity is clearly open to further interpretation. Whilst the categories of Pakistani and Bangladeshi are relatively unambiguous, Indian refers as much to nationality as ethnicity and varies according to religion, language and place of origin. In addition, the size of both the Other-Asian and the Other-Other (mostly of Arab or Middle Eastern descent) census categories (197,534 and 290,206 respectively), demonstrate how difficult it is to get a true picture of Britain's ethnic diversity.

The White Paper on the 2001 Census of Great Britain which sets out the format of the ethnic origin and religion questions has already been criticised for failing to foster a multicultural society. Antony Lerman and Professor Barry Kosmin of the Institute for Jewish Policy Research argue that the questions give the appearance of a preferred hierarchy of answers, 'as if the norm is "white Christian" and every other religious or ethnic category is a deviation from it' (Lerman and Kosmin, *The Guardian*, 1999). Lerman and Kosmin highlight the absurdity by which Chinese people are not categorised as Asian, which the pair describe as the result of an attempt 'to colour-code the population by a list system'.

Population and settlement estimates

The *1991 Census* showed approximately 1.5 million South Asians living in Britain, with a further 198,000 Asians listed as having 'other' origins. Ethnic minority communities (essentially non-Europeans) together comprise over 3 million, or 5.5 per cent of the UK population. As Table 1 shows, Indians constitute the largest ethnic minority community overall, numbering over 840,000. Pakistanis number 477,000 whilst Bangladeshis, although totalling just 163,000, are the youngest and fastest growing of all ethnic groups in the UK.

Whilst the vast bulk of Britain's West Indian population arrived prior to 1972, the influx of West Indians slowed progressively from as far back as the 1960s. In contrast, Asian men began to arrive after the West Indian migration began to decline, following the 1962 Commonwealth Immigrants Act. The pattern of settlement of different Asian groups and between men and women also varies. Around 10 per cent of Indian, Pakistani and Bangladeshi men arrived in Britain prior to 1960 and about 60 per cent by 1968. This period was then followed by the arrival of the majority of East African Asians, following Idi

15

Table 1

Size of Britain's ethnic minority communities (in descending order) in 1991 (Based on 1991 Census of Great Britain)

	Numbers	% of UK population
Indian	840,255	1.53
Black – Caribbean	499,964	0.91
Pakistani	476,555	0.87
Other – Other	290,206	0.53
Black – African	212,362	0.39
Other – Asian	197,534	0.36
Black – Other	178,401	0.33
Bangladeshi	162,835	0.30
Chinese	156,938	0.29

Reference: *Office for National Statistics, 1996*

Amin's expulsion of Asian people from Uganda in 1972. However, the mass of Indian migration pre-dated that of Pakistanis and Bangladeshis and the time lag between male and female entry was far shorter than for Pakistanis and Bangladeshis.

Conforming to these known patterns of immigration, the qualified figures in Table 2 shows the *estimated* rate of growth of the Indian, Pakistani and Bangladeshi populations between 1951 and 1991. If true, they confirm that Bangladeshis are the youngest and fastest growing population of all ethnic groups.

A controversial comparison

The economic and social experience of each main South Asian community has also varied dramatically, leading demographic commentator Ceri Peach controversially to liken the position of Britain's Indian community to a

Table 2

Estimated growth size and growth of Indian, Pakistani and Bangladeshi ethnic populations in Great Britain, 1951-1991*

	Indian	Pakistani	Bangladeshi
1951	31,000	10,000	2,000
1961	81,000	25,000	6,000
1966	223,000	64,000	11,000
1971	375,000	119,000	22,000
1981	676,000	296,000	65,000
1991	840,000	477,000	163,000

* 1991 census asked a question on ethnic origin for the first time; figures before this time are estimates only.

Source: **Ceri Peach, 1996**

'Jewish' model, and the Pakistani and Bangladeshi groupings to an 'Irish' model. 'The "Irish" model is seen as blue collar, manual labour dominated, council house tenured, inner city, whilst the "Jewish" model is seen as white collar, self-employed, owner-occupied and suburban' (*Ethnicity in the 1991 Census*, 1996). Whilst Britain's Indian community has achieved considerable economic success as a whole, rates of unemployment are significantly higher amongst Britain's Pakistani and Bangladeshi communities. By contrast, the Jewish community sector is now long established in Britain, with a large number of individual Jewish philanthropists and well-endowed trusts set up specifically or mainly to support Jewish causes.

At the latter end of the twentieth century the South Asian community sector is flourishing because it is similarly needs-led. Self-help groups amongst Southall's Asian community, for example, are extremely strong, but only, claims Harpal Brar, as a result of a complete disregard of community needs by the local council: 'The Conservatives didn't bother because they knew the Asians wouldn't vote for them and the Labour Party didn't bother either because they don't think they'll vote for anyone else.' (*Harpal Brar, law lecturer at the University of Westminster, interview with Zerbanoo Gifford*)

17

The Jewish experience

A community within a community

The Jewish voluntary sector in the UK today clearly sees itself as having a distinct identity, both in service and funding provision. In contrast to any so-called Asian voluntary sector, the Jewish voluntary sector clearly feels it has a definite target group largely uncomplicated by differences of culture, religion or belief.

The Institute of Jewish Policy Research is engaged in a wholesale review of the role and future of the Jewish voluntary sector in the UK. Its origins are not dissimilar to certain areas of the emerging Asian voluntary sector.

Often, the reasons cited for charitable giving reveal comparable preoccupations with religion, social responsibility, family tradition and, most of all, a realisation that the community's needs will only be fully met through self-help.

Interviews with charity donors in the United States contained in The Jewish Voluntary Sector, describe how charity and philanthropy have become an integral part of Jewish life. 'The Talmud, which is the written law, makes one feel very strongly about [charity] the fact that this is a guiding principle of our religion means that it is something that every Jewish child understands. They start out in their first Jewish educational experiences giving for some Jewish purpose. The reason that it is for Jewish purposes and why the Jewish community is so highly organised is because throughout our history we have always lived a little bit outside of the general society. It has been the feeling of both Jews and the general community that Jews must take care of their own needs.'

A European perspective

Charity is clearly a living phenomenon, no more a creation of the UK, the West or Judao-Christian tradition than of any other nation or religion. Diverse interpretations of what constitutes charity have hitherto hampered attempts by the European Commission to arrive at a workable definition. Examining the various manifestations of Europe's charitable sector, all that is really clear is that the UK's concept of charity is peculiarly British. Attempts to produce a cross-national analysis of the non-profit sector have thrown up palpable confusion about what the sector actually constitutes and whether a workable definition can cross national boundaries: 'the non-profit sector is poorly understood not so much because the data on it are so limited as because the concepts used to depict its boundaries are so murky and imprecise.' (*Defining the non-profit sector: a cross-national analysis*, 1997)

Outside Britain, particularly in Southern Europe, welfare and charity were for a long time almost exclusively the domain of the Catholic Church and in Italy were regulated by canon law. In France, where the State today still embodies the principles of the Social Contract, charity is principally over-shadowed by institutions; charitable giving is about a fifth of that in England. In Northern Europe, away from the all-pervading dominance of the Catholic Church, many of the conditions facilitating the UK notion of charity and philanthropy have prevailed. The public acceptance of private wealth is clearly a major factor in whether foundations and similar grant-making organisations will be established. It is also necessary for public opinion to endorse private philanthropy co-existing alongside the public provision of services, whilst tax incentives and limits on capital transfer and accumulation, though not regularly cited by philanthropists as a motivating force, undoubtedly play a part.

However in modern multicultural Britain the situation is different again. The immense contribution by a wide variety of cultures and religions, including the UK's South Asian communities, is altering our perspective and experience of charity. Originating in part from a context of diversity and discrimination, the UK's South Asian voluntary sector consists of a range of different groups, covering the whole spectrum of voluntary activity evident in the mainstream. It encompasses groups offering care services, advocacy, counselling and advice, arts, social welfare, employment, gay and lesbian projects, as well as numerous cultural, educational and religious organisations. Bahai, Buddhist, Christian, Hindu, Ismaili, Jain, Muslim, Sikh, Sindhi and Zoroastrian voluntary organisations are all active in the UK, going far beyond the conventional portrait of a white-dominated voluntary sector underpinned by Judao-Christian concepts of giving.

Responding to prejudice

The importance of religion to the various South Asian communities in Britain cannot be overestimated, not least because it has often provided vital support to marginalised communities. The significance in terms of charitable funding is also great, as many minority community voluntary organisations have their roots in religious organisations. A glance at the Charity Commission's database of the 180,000+ charities makes the above abundantly clear. The *Directory of Asian Voluntary Organisations* (Confederation of Indian Organisations, 1994/95) lists close to 150 organisations under its category of religion, though almost all offer a range of other services. These range from language classes and translation to advice on benefits, domestic violence, housing, immigration, counselling in short all that a community in late twentieth-century Britain might expect from well-run social services.

Despite the clear need for voluntary organisations offering these and count-less other services within many minority communities, charitable funders have often been guilty of putting their prejudices before their desire to support a particular charitable endeavour. As the Association of Charitable Foundations' 1996 report *Fairness in Funding* urges, trusts and other funders need to look beyond the surface of an application, if they are to successfully direct funding to projects aimed at Asian and other minority communities: 'Funding minority ethnic projects may necessitate looking for "hidden" barriers: if a foundation specifically precludes religious associations, it may find it impossible to reach some black communities, since the only way in which some minority ethnic groups are organised is via the local mosque, temple or synagogue' (*Fairness in Funding*, 1996).

'The voluntary sector is the means through which religious and other ethnic minorities can, in the field of social provision, sustain their own identities.' (*Wolfenden Report*)

As outlined above, there is little likelihood that Britain's South Asians will ever form a cohesive grouping, the split along religious lines proving too strong. A broad division has also emerged between the differing economic and social experiences of the main South Asian communities in Britain. Britain's South Asian Muslims, originating largely from Pakistan and Bangladesh, have to a large degree experienced social and economic marginalisation. Britain's largely Hindu Indian population, on the other hand, has been more economically successful. Asking the question 'Why have Indians been so successful in British society?' the South Asian Development Partnership suggested two reasons: 'First, their success could have much to do with the fact that a high proportion of Indians now in the UK came from a middle-class background. Second, their academic/success-oriented culture may fit more easily into British society than the rural/agrarian cultures of their Pakistani and Bangladeshi counterparts.' (*South Asian Population Report for Great Britain*, 1992). A third possibility is that a host of religious prejudices have allowed certain cultures to be more readily accepted than others. More than any other black and minority community in the UK, Britain's Muslim community has most recently borne the brunt of ingrained prejudices.

Fundamentalism, Jihad, and Fatwa are terms easily associated by the West with Islam and each is laden with a myriad of explosive prejudices. By contrast, little is known about Zakat, the 'charity tax', which requires a 2.5 per cent tithe from all Muslims, and the all-embracing tolerance of a religion which in the UK has 1.2 million adherents. Grant-making trusts established by Muslims in the UK are also gaining ground with a number offering significant levels of funding to both Muslim and non-Muslim causes.

The origins of South Asian Muslims in the UK

Zakat

Helping others, or 'zakat', is one of the five pillars of Islam, along with prayers, fasting, pilgrimage and declaration of faith. Placing a compulsory requirement on Muslims to pay over 2.5 per cent of income it is perhaps more akin to a tax than charity. In Pakistan, the government collects zakat directly from individuals.

The position of Muslims in the UK has been likened to that of Irish Catholics in the nineteenth century. When the first substantial influx of Muslim immigrants arrived in the 1970s, they were subjected to prejudices similar to those experienced by the Irish before. Largely a male population to begin with, they lived in isolation, the first generation apparently more interested in looking back to the 'old country' where they thought they would return when they had made their fortune. Politics for British Muslims was apparently more concerned with the situation in Pakistan than in Britain and in 1970 a candidate for the Pakistan People's Party stood in the local council elections in Bradford. Language and cultural barriers limited contact and even when families began to take root they were still seen as forming an 'awkward minority', as Irish Catholics had done in the past, neither wanting to live completely separately nor to completely integrate. Unlike other communities of immigrants, not all Muslims in Britain have been prepared to be integrated solely on the dominant culture's terms. Muslim schools and calls for a separate Muslim parliament demonstrate the widespread disquiet of Britain's Muslims.

When Sheikh Dr Zaki Badawi gave the 1996 Association of Charitable Foundations annual lecture on philanthropy, he referred to the 'Islamaphobia' now sweeping Western Europe and all too readily made manifest in the media. 'Although Prince Charles didn't say one word about mosques, even when he made a statement the other day about architecture, the *Daily Mail* came out with the front page headline, *Charles calls for building Mosques*. Why Mosques for goodness sake? All the man said was, "Let's build religious institutions for all and let's consider religious communities as well." ' (ACF Third Annual Lecture on Philanthropy, 1996)

'Philanthropy is not about housing for refugees, or support for elderly, it's about empowering people and changing their lives.' (*Vikram Shah, academic, interview with Zerbanoo Gifford*)

Although charity and the Mosque are clearly linked in Islam, there are now many major grant-making charities with Muslim connections clearly not giving either through or to the mosque. Unlike other national grant-making trusts, many of these charities, including Muslim Aid, Islamic Relief, Human Relief and Muslim Hands, have a strong non-religious regional base and in many cases present a model of how philanthropy can be community- and grassroots-based.

> 'Charity for Muslims is not just about alleviating suffering, but also about education as the latter helps prevent the former from occurring.' (*Mohammed Akbar Ali, interview with Zerbanoo Gifford*)

Likewise there are strong traditions of philanthropy amongst Britain's other South Asian communities based in part on their religious heritage, ranging from Jainism's Ban (literally, giving it away) to the Zoroastrian ethical triad of good thought, word and deed; from the five pillars of Islam to the Hindu principles of Karma.

> 'If everyone was fortunate enough to be able to give to charity, then who needs it?'
>
> 'I often tell my English friends, "you could live in a village in Gujerat for a year and no one would ask you for the money for your food." So now who is poor?'
>
> 'We live a highly contradictory life. We know we have Hindu blood in our veins, but lamely try to imitate the English and say we are as good as them.'
>
> 'Our god says enjoy life and enjoy wealth, but give it away too' (*Vikram Shah, academic, interview with Zerbanoo Gifford*)

Whilst some religions may emphasise the need to give to charity in order to attain spiritual fulfilment, philanthropy has often played a far more corporeal role, allowing marginalised or minority communities to retain their cohesion. The Zoroastrians have a long and proud tradition of charitable giving both within and outside their own community. Traditionally wealthy wherever they have settled, they have also tended to be in a minority throughout their history whether in India, South Africa, East Africa or most recently in the UK.

> 'Religious tolerance is also a form of philanthropy' (*Rusi Dalal, President of Zoroastrian Trust Funds of Europe, interview with Zerbanoo Gifford*)

Historically, the Zoroastrians controlled great trade empires ensuring not only closer links with other communities, but a need to gain credence with other cultures in order to grow and survive.

Although the days of the merchant princes are long gone and with them most of the big Zoroastrian philanthropists, in India many testaments to their success remain. In the UK, ranging from the late Freddie Mercury to a large number of philanthropists who remain fiercely anonymous, Zoroastrians continue their own tradition of a broad range of giving both within their community and in support of wider society.

> 'Charity is part of our religious and cultural heritage. To collect wealth and distribute it.' (*Rusi Dalal, President of Zoroastrian Trust Funds of Europe, interview with Zerbanoo Gifford*)

Smashing the glass ceiling

Making an impact in the voluntary sector

Despite Sondhi and Salmon's words (see below), on the eve of the new millennium race issues are back at the top of the agenda and racism is firmly with us. The Macpherson Report on the Stephen Lawrence Inquiry lays bare the 'pernicious and institutionalised racism' rife within the Metropolitan Police. The 335-page report has been described as a watershed for the eradication of institutional racism and may well herald new powers given to the Commission of Racial Equality.

> ### Institutional racism
>
> '... the collective failure of an organisation to provide an appropriate professional service to people because of their colour, culture or ethnic origin.' (*Sir William Macpherson, Stephen Lawrence Inquiry report*)

Over a hundred years ago there were three Asian MPs in Britain. In today's multicultural Britain, there are just five Asian MPs, elected to parliament on 1 May 1997: Piara Khabra, Ashok Kumar, Mohammad Sarwar, Marsha Singh and Keith Vaz. Even coupled with the four black MPs currently sitting, all nine representing Labour, it is a depressingly low figure, particularly in the light of New Labour's landslide and apparently groundbreaking victory which elevated both more women and a younger generation into government.

'The 1980s opened with race high on the domestic agenda. In comparison, the 1990s have opened quietly, and race issues have slid down the agenda. That, alas, does not mean that the issues have gone away, or that racism has been purged from the system.' (*Race, racism and local authorities, 1992*)

The Prime Minister himself raised the issue of the absence of minority communities from positions of power in his speech at the 1997 Labour Party conference. Cabinet Office figures at the time showed just two black or Asian people in the top four grades of the civil service and just 58 among the next 3,000 policy-makers. A recent listing compiled by Channel 4 and *The Observer* newspaper of the 300 most powerful people in UK media, politics, arts, science and business contained just three Asians.

Virtually all areas of public life are similarly lacking in adequate South Asian and black representation, other than in economically and politically powerless positions or individual successes as sportsmen or entertainers – and this despite the high proportion of professions which have long had a large number of South Asians within them.

The lack of black people employed in the media is staggering. There are estimated to be between 12 and 20 non-whites among the roughly 5,000 journalists on national newspapers (between 0.24 and 0.40 per cent), whilst provincial newspapers have only 15 non-whites amongst 8,000 journalists (just 0.18 per cent). In broadcasting, where there are considerably more initiatives targeting people from black and minority communities, approximately 300 non-whites are employed in editorial jobs (based on information contained in *The Observer*, 7 July 1996).

There are some notable exceptions. Twenty years ago just 1 per cent of magistrates were from black and minority communities, today this has risen to a more respectable 6 per cent; whilst 10 per cent of the board of prison visitors are from black and minority communities. However, the lack of balanced media coverage of minority communities means there is a consistent failure to reflect on the successes of these communities outside their stereotypical roles as sportsmen or entertainers – or criminals! As the meteoric rise of the Ugandan Asian middle classes demonstrates, there is much professional, social and economic progress. However this heartening tale of minority community success in mainstream Britain was reported in *The Asian Times*, not *The Sunday Times* and certainly not the *Daily Mail*.

Unfortunately, despite the broad spectrum of many thousands of voluntary organisations working within black and minority communities, the voluntary sector is no enlightened exception. Despite the strong presence of a vibrant

> Ugandan Asians, who came to Britain as refugees in 1972, have been trans-
> formed from 'pariahs to paragons', according to immigration experts.
>
> Now their successes comprehensively eclipse the performance of white
> Britons. Statistics show that 26 per cent are self-employed compared to 16
> per cent of whites and as employees, their rise has been still more startling. In
> 1981, only 6 per cent of Ugandan Asian women were managers. Ten years
> later, the figure was 24 per cent, just 1 per cent behind white women.
> Among males, 37 per cent of Ugandan Asian men are managers compared
> with 28 per cent of white men.' (*'Refugees rise rapidly into the middle
> classes', Asian Times, 13 January 1996*)

heterogeneity of South Asian voluntary organisations, they remain part of a marginalised sector subsumed under an inappropriate umbrella with black organisations and groups representing other minority communities. The mainstream white voluntary sector, despite the rhetoric of engagement with South Asian communities, is explicitly failing to meet their needs.

Mythical South Asian women and the reality

The stereotyped perception of South Asian communities in the UK is nowhere stronger than in the view of South Asian women. From images of socialite wives organising charity balls for causes 'back home', to young Muslim girls suicidal because of forced arranged marriages, the stereotypes are obviously riddled with contradictions.

> 'For an Asian woman having given so much within the family, just giving a lit-
> tle to charity is no real effort' (*Vanita Patel, interview with Zerbanoo
> Gifford*)

The suicide rate amongst young South Asian women is undoubtedly high, but is actually higher amongst Hindus than Muslims. And whilst there are evidently many wealthy South Asian women, engaged in organising elaborate fundraising functions, the rapidly growing number of professional South Asian women goes virtually unnoticed.

'The media always appears to focus on the tragic consequences of being an Asian woman in the West; mental health problems, suicide and forced marriages do exist, as they do in many other communities, but they are only a small part of our experience.' (*Telling It Like It Is*, 1997)

Kassam's book offers an alternative view of young British Asian women, moving profoundly away from that described by Vanita Patel (quoted above). The experiences documented in *Telling It Like It Is* reflect those of largely third generation young South Asian women, no less rooted in the extended family typical of South Asian community life but for whom being a South Asian woman is neither a punishment nor a restriction.

One way traffic

'Mainstream charities tend to think how can we tap into this area of money rather than how can we involve and engage this charity in our work.' (*Usha Prashar, former director NCVO, interview with Zerbanoo Gifford*)

The attitude of the majority of mainstream voluntary organisations towards the involvement of black and minority communities is epitomised by a recent paper published in the *Journal of Non-profit and Voluntary Sector Marketing*. Arguing that a significant opportunity for tapping into a rich source of funding awaits the right fundraising approach, *UK Asian Communities: a profitable market for non-profits* points to the growing role played by South Asian communities in the UK, whilst questioning the lack of financial and hands-on involvement by South Asians in the mainstream voluntary sector. 'Asian communities are rapidly becoming significant players in UK society, and the market has great potential from the charity viewpoint. It is highly identifiable, there is a strong tradition of philanthropy; it has increasing economic power, is accessible and has a sense of social responsibility' (*Journal of Non-profit and Voluntary Sector Marketing* Volume 2, 1997). Likewise the South Asian Development Partnership, a registered charity looking to increase the participation of South Asians in mainstream British society, refer to the '£5 billion opportunity', the estimated disposable income of UK's South Asian population. Aside from their work with charities and the development of South Asian philanthropy, the South Asian Development Partnership is involved in providing information to government and the corporate sector who are increasingly looking to tap into the UK's South Asian market.

Charities working within the mainstream voluntary sector, just like other less socially responsible sectors of society, have long been guilty of neglecting their potential donor base. It is perhaps not surprising, if a little sad, that the ever-competitive fight for charitable funding is at last forcing mainstream charities to sit up and look at their appeal to black and minority communities.

However, there is a considerable amount of work still to be done. The lack of black and Asian representation in the large charities is acute, at every level. From staffing to management committee and trustee representation, the white, essentially middle-class bias of the UK's voluntary sector, still prevails. NCVO's 1994 *Building on Trust* report revealed that 95 per cent of all trustees are white. The situation amongst other bodies, closely related to the voluntary sector, quangos, Local Authority commissioning boards, grant-making trusts, etc., except where there have been positive initiatives to correct the situation, is even more extreme.

In order to address their lack of success and involvement in meeting the needs of Britain's South Asian communities, mainstream voluntary organisations need to look beyond mere tokenism if they are to have any chance of gaining both the respect and the economic support of South Asian communities. As a recent Confederation of Indian Organisations research report outlined: 'It was clear that on the whole mainstream organisations did not have policies or strategies to address the specific development needs of South Asian organisations ... It is easy for agencies to fall into the trap of employing one worker to deal with the ethnic communities and then the rest of the staff and management abdicate their responsibilities to these communities. It is essential that where an agency has a genuine concern to provide support for ethnic organisations, that there are appropriate policies, structures and services in place to allow them to deliver meaningful services.'

Who should meet the needs?

Notwithstanding the onus on mainstream organisations to better target their services to meet the needs of Asian communities, there is also an argument that South Asian voluntary organisations are best placed for this task. As the *Black Voluntary Sector Manifesto* noted: 'Black groups are best placed to deliver services to their own communities and should not have to compete with white groups to meet the service needs of their own communities.' It appears that in many areas, mainstream voluntary organisations and statutory agencies are comprehensively failing to meet the needs of South Asian people.

'People have to identify with causes beyond their community. Integration for me will be when everyone is rattling a collection box together.' (*Navnit Dholakia, interview with Zerbanoo Gifford*)

Recent research into the housing and mental health care needs of South Asian people in the London boroughs of Brent/Harrow, Ealing and Tower Hamlets was severely critical of the level of services available to South Asian people. The research, published by the Joseph Rowntree Foundation, found that myths and stereotypes about South Asian people dominate the thinking of both professionals and policy-makers. It revealed that too few services are aimed specifically at South Asian people with mental health problems and that there is an urgent need for appropriate housing, help with independent living skills, advice on housing and welfare benefits, counselling in Asian languages and a host of advocacy-related activities. South Asian people reported feeling isolated from and neglected by the professional services and the study urged 'mainstream services to be more sensitive to cultural issues' and to develop a range of services to meet the identified needs of Asian people with mental health problems (Joseph Rowntree Foundation Finding No. 79, 1996).

> 'There is still a lot of racism within companies and organisations and this does prevent Asians from making their way to positions of influence. Laws only change things to a minor extent. You have to change people's attitudes in the day to day reality, so they can see why it is important to have fair representation. Role models change structures.' (*Kamlesh Bahl, former Chair, Equal Opportunities Commission, interview with Zerbanoo Gifford*)

A recent analysis of the operation of the UK voluntary sector at a local level commented on how 'the black voluntary sector has blazed the trail in identifying unmet needs, in developing appropriate and relevant services and in local capacity building' (*Dimensions of the Voluntary Sector, 1998*). With the mainstream voluntary sector clearly failing to meet the diverse needs of the many minority communities, the importance of the black voluntary sector cannot be overestimated.

Funding – a minority activity

There has been no comprehensive research into the funding of either the South Asian voluntary sector or the black and minority community voluntary sector as a whole, despite suggestions that the sector now consists of over 40,000 voluntary and community groups. However, despite the sector's size and importance, as yet there have not been any significant breakthroughs into the fundraising big league. As an overview on the funding of voluntary organisations at local level notes, 'it is clear that such organisations do not feature among the wealthiest charities, tending generally to have low incomes' (*Dimensions of the Voluntary Sector, 1998*).

> 'The crisis in funding is more acute with organisations in this sector than in any other sector' (*Confederation of Indian Organisations, unpublished report into the funding of the Asian voluntary sector, 1996*)

Several published statistics reveal the extent to which the black and minority community voluntary sector is the poor relation of its wealthy white competitors. The 1997/98 handbook of the Association of Chief Executives in National Organisations (ACENVO) includes no black organisations with an annual income of over £5 million in a listing of 127 organisations.

Whilst equal opportunities practice has come on leaps and bounds in recent years, in one highly significant area it has been comprehensively disregarded. Charitable funders, whilst often propounding principles of public accountability and helping those in greatest need, are generally falling way short of the minimum now acceptable in much of corporate Britain.

'Procedures that are now taken for granted in fair employment practice – open competition, and specification and short-listing on merit, for example – are notably absent in the grant-making practice of many funders, whether public bodies, companies, or trusts and foundations.' (*Dimensions of the Voluntary Sector, 1997*)

South Asian voluntary organisations are relatively new arrivals to the voluntary sector and have a variety of specific needs and characteristics often overlooked by funders. There has been limited research into the voluntary organisations that serve South Asian communities in Britain and the nature of the funding they receive. However, a report compiled in 1996 by the Confederation of Indian Organisations asserted the unique nature of what it termed the 'Asian voluntary sector': 'such community-based organisations cannot be found within the indigenous community' (CIO, 1996).

The limited research into the funding of the black and minority community voluntary sector has indicated how many voluntary organisations run by and for black and minority communities are financially relatively self-sufficient, if by necessity: 'The largest source of funding for a whole range of small groups is the local Black community itself' (*Funding Black Groups*, 1992).

The status quo

In 1996, the Confederation of Indian Organisations (CIO) undertook an extensive research programme into the South Asian voluntary sector, its infrastructure, support and development needs and the impact of changes in funding policies and practices. Of the 1,000 organisations canvassed, including South Asian voluntary organisations, funders and umbrella organisations, a total of 180 responses were received.

The results make stark reading. Virtually 50 per cent of respondents received no external funding at all, aside from income received from their respective communities through donations, subscription fees and local fundraising. Despite this, local community support and involvement can produce astounding results: 'A clear example of this spirit of giving back to the community, self-help and mobilising community members for the common goal for the good of the community was seen in the building of the Swaminarayan Temple in Neasden, London. This brought together the community where each individual volunteered their skills and expertise. Solicitors took care of the legal work, architects of the design, builders and carpenters volunteered their free services to build the temple. This resulted in an amazing construction for the community. This example can be found in all religious communities.' (CIO, 1996)

Taking into account the range of services provided by these organisations and the absence of any alternative provision, the CIO report notes: 'It is important for those in positions of power to take a step back and reflect on what would be the monetary cost of replacing the input of these unfunded organisations and the human cost for communities if such organisations did not exist for them.' However it was also evident that whilst local community support was essential for the continuing financial viability of many organisations, external economic pressures meant that in Britain's most disadvantaged areas local community support was proving harder to obtain.

The financial instability of the South Asian voluntary organisations managing to secure external funding was also marked. 60 per cent of groups receiving outside funding were reliant on annual grants, only 18 per cent of organisations securing three yearly grants. Core funding had only been obtained by 20 per cent of funded organisations.

Funding by Local Authorities

Whilst the relationship between Local Authorities and voluntary organisations generally has changed considerably over recent years, its negative effects have been most acutely felt within the black and minority community voluntary sector. Cuts to available funding, coupled with a change in philosophy redefining Local Authorities as purchasers, enablers and commissioners of services, have impacted severely on this new and emerging sector: 'as the Black voluntary sector as a whole is relatively new and many groups are small and inexperienced, the effects of these cuts is probably more pronounced with longer term effects, than in any other part of the voluntary sector' (*Funding Black Groups*, 1992).

Despite the shift in the funding relationship, Local Authorities still provide the principle source of funding to South Asian voluntary organisations, as with many other local community-based voluntary groups. As the CIO report

Funding of the South Asian Voluntary Sector

A unique sector

Particular problems faced by black and ethnic minority voluntary organisations, are that they:

– Are under-resourced and tend to be small and community based, with poor access to funds and support and with few national network bodies.

– Have been set up in response to racism, in order to deal with it, and to provide resources not being provided by the state, the private sector or traditional voluntary organisations.

– Use informal, local networking, building on individual contacts, rather than relying upon formal organisational structures to develop joint work.

– Experience discrimination when negotiating, and some local groups have found that negotiation with power brokers only comes about as a result of conflict.

– Find that there are few mechanisms for negotiating differences within the black voluntary sector.

– Are under great pressure to resolve conflict out of the public eye, away from all too-ready criticism. This pressure results in many Black groups not being able to resolve conflict in a constructive way, as might happen in other groups.

– Bear great pressure to develop traditional organisational structures by funders. These structures may impede, or be in conflict with, the aims and objectives of the organisation.

– Find it difficult to recruit management committee members with the full range of skills and time available to manage organisations. Black people with skills in personnel, book-keeping, fundraising, etc., are in great demand by local groups, and with little training and support available for them to acquire these skills it means that Black groups often have to struggle to learn management skills on the job.

(taken from London Borough Grants Committee Sectoral Review, 1992)

notes, this makes groups, 'very vulnerable because they have no other source of funding that can buffer any effects of the tightening expenditure and resulting cuts in LA funding.'

The consultation exercises held by Local Authorities aimed at establishing the needs of local communities have often excluded South Asian communities. Under-representation of South Asians on local policy-making committees has resulted in the needs of the local South Asian communities being inadequately represented and, as a consequence, inadequately funded. In certain cases this has left the needs of South Asian communities completely unmet, largely because of a complete lack of cultural sensitivity by the Local Authority funder. 'One Local Authority funding department funded a Muslim group to provide a luncheon club for the elders. As this was the only luncheon club funded for Asians in the borough, the community voiced their concerns that there were no provisions for the Hindu community in the borough. The funding department subsequently asked the group to expand its services to serve elders from all the South Asian communities. However, this created huge difficulties as the vegetarian Hindus wanted the food to be cooked in a separate facility and did not want meat near their food; similarly the Muslim elders would not eat food cooked by Hindu staff. Ultimately the funding department ceased funding to the group. This has left the elders with no facilities.' (CIO, 1996)

South Asian voluntary organisations face additional problems securing funding from Local Authorities because of the move from grant aid, given to selected organisations, to Service Led Agreements, where grants are judged strictly on the level of *service* being offered. Whilst a number of the issues raised by this seismic shift in the relationship between Local Authorities and community organisations apply across the board, as outlined above, small Asian voluntary organisations are marked by a tendency to offer a range of services, rendering them holistic by nature and insufficiently quantifiable or cost-efficient. As the CIO report notes: 'This method of funding places little value on additional services which are not easily quantifiable such as general advice and information, bhajans and other religious sessions, informal talks, showing videos and card games as well as communal cooking all of which have been meaningful activities often bringing together isolated individuals in the community.'

Central Government funding

Cuts in the central government funding of voluntary organisations have also had a particularly negative impact on the black and Asian voluntary sectors. So too has the centralising of funding initiatives which followed the axing of the Greater London Council. With the demise of the GLC in London so too went a multitude of funding programmes targeting black and minority communities. These were succeeded by various funding initiatives, including the Urban Programme, City Challenge, the Ethnic Minority Grant and Ethnic Minority Business Initiative, which have all since been subsumed into the Single Regeneration Budget. The Single Regeneration Budget, based on the principle that services offered by mainstream organisations should be accessible to minority communities in general, ended the ring-fenced funding specifically targeted at minority community organisations. A new emphasis on regional government and a mayor for London may herald a new direction.

There remain areas of government funding which whilst not remaining unscathed by sweeping changes have been at least alert to the detrimental effects of cuts on the black and minority community voluntary sector. The London Borough Grants Committee, in its sectoral review of Black and Asian Groups in 1992 noted that against a backdrop of worsening social and economic conditions for London's black and minority communities: 'the Committee's funding to Black and Asian groups has actually fallen in real terms. It is therefore imperative that over time the Committee redresses this situation and develops a strategy that targets its resources more generously on these communities so that they themselves tackle the problems which face them' (LBGC, 1992). That said, despite clear good attentions, the outcome of the review was additional funding to black and Asian groups totalling just £10,080 in 1992/93, rising to £40,320 in 1993/94.

Trust funding

As detailed above, trust funding of black and Asian groups is minimal, although there are signs that trusts are increasingly being set up by Asians which in some cases specifically target Asian community organisations. The Confederation of Indian Organisations' survey of its members found that just 5 per cent (8 from 180 respondents) had received any funding at all from trusts, a lamentable situation. As the report notes, 'Funding from trusts has remained a largely untapped source for Asian voluntary organisations.' The various changes to accessing statutory funding sources detailed above and the detrimental effect on South Asian voluntary organisations will inevitably increase the already heavy demand on grant-making trusts. It is imperative that trusts recognise this situation and make allowances accordingly to increase support of minority community organisations.

National Lottery funding

Despite immense controversy from its inception to the present day, the National Lottery has been the runaway revenue-raising success predicted by its camp followers. Of the five bodies originally set up to co-ordinate the distribution of the National Lottery's charity proceeds, the National Lottery Charities Board, endorsing its commitment to help those at greatest disadvantage and to improve the quality of life in the community, has by far exceeded its partner bodies in its commitment to funding equality. (It has in fact bettered virtually all of its statutory and voluntary partner funding bodies.) Research published by the National Lottery Charities Board in 1997 states, 'By February 1997, the NLCB had disbursed a total of £478 million in 6,925 grants to voluntary organisations. Of that sum, approximately £52 million, or 11 per cent, was awarded to projects working principally with minority ethnic communities.' (*Dimensions of the Voluntary Sector 1997*.)

Of this £52 million of grants disbursed, a sizeable proportion has been specifically targeted at organisations run by people from minority ethnic groups, defined by the NLCB as projects where people from minority ethnic groups form over half the management committee, as well as those run on behalf of, although not necessarily by, specific minority communities.

Whilst the National Lottery Charities Board is exemplary for its targeted support of black and other minority ethnic community organisations, the four other lottery distributors are notable for not compiling an ethnic breakdown of funds distributed. The recently established New Opportunities Fund (the sixth good cause) looks like it may well follow the path of the National Lottery Charities Board, in its adherence to good practice.

The way forward

There is clearly an aching need within the South Asian voluntary sector for support services. However, this in itself is problematic. The CIO notes that: 'It is dubious whether there can be "one voice" for the many organisations that form the [South Asian] voluntary sector ... where issues concern the Asian community, such as the wearing of turbans for Sikh schoolchildren, the closing of the Hare Krishna temple, grant maintained status for Muslim schools, there is a lack of mainstream representation.'

It is unlikely that a support organisation offering services to all non-white voluntary and community groups would have widespread backing, with South Asian groups calling for more distinct representation, as evidenced by the CIO research: 'Groups identify with an Asian organisation more than an organisation set up to serve all the minority communities under the generic term 'black'. The respondents felt that an Asian organisation would 'be better able to understand the needs and issues of our client groups' (CIO report, 1996).

Additionally, the historical failure of mainstream voluntary organisations to represent adequately the needs of South Asian groups appear to have terminally damaged their credibility for any future representation. 'Having excluded Asian organisations from their service delivery, membership, mailing lists as well as consultation exercises, mainstream agencies could not then claim to be able to represent them or the needs of their users.' (CIO report, 1996)

The business of philanthropy

Early in 1997 the magazine *Eastern Eye* published *Britain's Richest Asian 100*, a groundbreaking piece of research which finally announced publicly and to a mainstream audience that South Asians are now part of the UK establishment and are here to stay.

'The retail concentration was highlighted in a survey by Mars, the confectionery maker. It revealed that by the early 1990s Asians owned 95 per cent of all independently owned shops (excluding multiples) within the area ringed by the M25 in south-east England, Nationally the figure was 65 per cent. And 78 per cent of the independent retail sector was controlled by Gujeratis.' (*'Britain's Richest Asian 100', Eastern Eye, April 1997*)

Philip Beresford (editor of the *Sunday Times Richest 1,000*), in his commentary to the piece, revealed, 'It tells an extraordinary story. The proverbial and enduring qualities of thrift, hard work, and self-sacrifice underpin this quiet revolution. It has transformed many little corners and high streets throughout Britain; it has ushered in a new food culture; it has produced a millionaire class confident of its wealth; and finally, it has proved more enduring than the enterprise culture of Thatcherism, the political philosophy which most closely approximates to Asian values.'

In 1998 and 1999 *Eastern Eye* built significantly on its inaugural list expanding it to cover the richest 200 South Asians in Britain, whose collective fortunes are estimated at £7.5 billion. Not only does the compilation of a 'rich list' underline the growing awareness of the wealth of UK Asians and their businesses (the top five South Asian families alone are together valued at virtually £3.5 billion – see Table 3), but it also gives notice, albeit just a glimpse, of how charitable funding in the UK and overseas is set to be transformed in the next millennium.

Both the 1998 and 1999 listings of Britain's richest 200 Asians underline the economic prowess of many individual South Asians. The 'brown pound', as

35

Eastern Eye chooses to name it, has become an economic necessity in many British cities.

In 1994, the book *The Millionaire Givers* had presented for the first time a breakdown of the charitable giving of over 270 of the UK's wealthiest individuals. Just a handful of South Asians were included in the listing, namely Swraj Paul, Raj Bagri, the Hinduja brothers, Nat Puri and Lakshmi Shivdasani, only serving to underline the reluctance of not only the business world but also the voluntary sector to afford them equal status. Clearly the reality was somewhat different. It was not that there were no wealthy South Asians, as *Eastern Eye*'s recent publications have amply demonstrated, nor that these individuals were not involved in philanthropic activity. The methods of giving might not conform to the way in which charity is traditionally dished out by business people in Britain, but the philanthropic transfer of cash was undoubtedly going on.

> 'When a large number of people arrive in another country to improve themselves, the first priority is to establish a good economic base. This takes a couple of decades. By the 1980s we began to hear of Asian businesses which were successful. The 1990s should have been the age when Asian businesses started to give money.' (*Shiv Sharma, Editor India Mail, interview with Zerbanoo Gifford*)

If charitable funding by wealthy South Asian individuals and their companies is even more of an opaque area than that of their white counterparts, it is perhaps partly a reflection of the British establishment's own prejudice. The City has been slow to welcome South Asian-owned businesses, as have South Asians been suspicious of perceived City interference or the corporate world's prejudices. It is notable that there is only one listed company in *Eastern Eye*'s *Britain's Richest Asian 100* in 1997, and the 1998 edition notes countless decisions from the heads of successful private Asian businesses to step back from possible flotation. In its most recent rich listing (1999) *Eastern Eye* notes that many Asian-owned businesses are being forced to contemplate stockmarket flotation, to relinquish control in order to grow. Despite past setbacks Asian-owned companies are, as the magazine states, 'in effect being pushed and pulled to change'. However the younger generation of Asians now controlling many major companies are thought to be well up to the challenge, and are perhaps best placed to challenge the British business establishment head on.

Ups and downs in the 1990s

The 1990s began badly for the UK's South Asian business population. The fall of BCCI (the Bank of Credit and Commerce International) in June 1991 not only damaged confidence, but financially crippled many small South Asian businessmen and charities who had invested in the multi-national banking corporation. It was also not a good time to be assessing the impact Asians might make to charitable funding.

'If you have one penny buy bread, if you have two pennies buy bread and a flower. One will tell you how to live and the other will tell you why to live.' (*Chinese proverb, quoted by Shiv Sharma, Editor India Mail, interview with Zerbanoo Gifford*)

The collapsed Bank of Credit and Commerce International was also intricately connected to a multi-million dollar network of foundations established in the UK, Pakistan and the Cayman Islands by the Bank's founder, Agha Hasan Abedi. The principle UK-registered grant-making trust, the ICIC Foundation, held an 8.4 per cent stake in BCCI Holdings in Luxembourg, the holding company of the banking group. The foundation's shares in 1989, just a year prior to the group's demise, were valued at $200 million. The UK-registered Third World Foundation for Social and Economic Studies was also one of the foundations at the forefront of BCCI's charitable work. It supported a range of periodicals on Third World issues including the *Third World Quarterly*, as well as establishing the Third World Prize worth $100,000, which has been awarded to Willy Brandt, Winnie and Nelson Mandela and Bob Geldof. Other grant makers within BCCI's world-wide foundation network included: the Pakistan-based BCCI Foundation, which spent many millions on health and welfare projects and slum improvement; the BCCI Foundation for the Advancement of Science and Technology; and the Cayman Islands-registered ICIC Staff Benevolent Fund. (Based on a report in *Trust Monitor*, 1991.)

When the bank crashed, so did an array of world-wide grant-making foundations which hitherto had appeared to signal to the world the arrival of both large-scale South Asian business and correspondingly extensive philanthropic involvement. Nearing the end of the decade it appears that confidence has risen once more. This is despite the recent collapse of plans by a group of twenty UK-based South Asian businessmen to launch an Asian bank with the Midland, part of the HSBC group which forms the largest financial services group in the world. The members of this collective, which include the Hinduja brothers, Lakshmi Mittal, Manubhai Madhvani, Lord Bagri and GK Noon, contain not only some of the most influential figures in the Asian business world, but also some of its most high profile philanthropists. City institutions at last look to be warming to successful Asian businesses whom they have long held at arm's length. Recent City appointments, including the meteoric rise of Jayesh Manek, who launched his own unit trust fund at the end of the 1997, have brought South Asians and the City at least under the same glass ceiling, even if the cracks are yet to show.

Trust initiatives

Historically, one of the by-products of large-scale wealth has been the establishment of grant-making trusts or foundations. The motives are many, including the extremes of self-grandiosity or a belief in social change (which inspired the founders of many of Britain's most innovative foundations). 'The memory of that three weeks' journey remained in Joseph's mind until he died. He saw half-dead women sitting by the roadside clutching dead babies. He saw men who lay dying beside a basket of turf which they had carried for miles and failed to sell. He saw places where the dead, uncoffined and unknown, had been laid in trenches by those too weak to do more. The schoolboy ... looked and remembered. It was his first encounter with destitution, and it was a landmark in his life.' (*A Quaker Business Man – The Life of Joseph Rowntree*)

More recently the motive for establishing trusts has come from advantageous tax breaks associated with giving to charity, with control of the use of money through trust giving. It is no surprise that the shift away from direct taxation during the Thatcher years coincided with an increased setting up of trusts.

Are wealthy South Asians setting up foundations?

Whilst rich people in Britain may not be hugely generous – recent estimates suggest that the 'super rich' as a group (excluding the exceptional George Soros) donated just 0.13 per cent of their net wealth (*The Millionaire Givers*) – many are associated with charitable trusts. The UK's South Asian population is certainly no exception, but, as Table 3 shows, some wealthy South Asians are choosing to set up charitable foundations as a route for their giving. However, this is not the whole picture. Just as various parts of the South Asian business world are at a relatively early point in their development in the UK, so it appears is South Asian philanthropy. Now that the economic basis has been laid, there will be pressure on those that have been successful to give more.

Amongst the high-profile donors there is certainly no clear pattern of giving. Some have chosen to give within a small area or within a particular community, whilst others have chosen to ally their giving to more general areas of support. Lord Paul's £1 million grant to London Zoo was notable for the widespread media interest it generated. Clearly it was an immensely generous act, but it was also made by a then relatively unknown (and South Asian) businessman.

'Now that we have made money and we're living in fancy houses and our children are educated, it's time to plough money back into the country.' (*Gulam Noon, businessman, interview with Zerbanoo Gifford*)

Some organisations have been quick to seize on the potential of new areas of funding support, including two organisations promoting the establishment of charitable trusts. The UK Charitable Trusts Initiative and the South Asian Development Partnership have both been involved in projects seeking to encourage wealthy South Asian individuals to establish grant–making trusts, with some, if limited, success. The UK Charitable Trusts Initiative has been behind the establishment of 100 new foundations since it was set up in 1990 representing £95 million of new money to the voluntary sector. As yet, initial

The Pukaar Foundation

A lesson in developing philanthropy

The Pukaar Foundation was established by QED Bradford Ltd (Quest for Education and Development), a charity launched in 1990 to help develop initiatives aimed largely at young Asian people. The Pukaar Foundation sprang from the charity's belief that it is important for wealthy individuals from the Asian community to invest something back.

Initial results have been disappointing. Launched early in 1997, the first efforts to raise money from Bradford's Asian business community raised between £8,000 and £9,000. Earlier hopes for a sum sufficient to provide an income-producing endowment have been put on hold. Despite a clear wish amongst Bradford's, predominantly Muslim, Asians to help their own communities, the fundraising efforts appear to have hit three principle stumbling blocks:

– wealthy Asians don't feel there is real poverty in the UK

– money that is given to charity tends to return to the Indian sub-continent

– the established method of Bradford's Muslim community receiving money has been very 'ad hoc'.

Initial grants have included £125 to the Tigre Trust which works with disadvantaged communities in Africa; £200 to an inner city farm; and £300 to Bradford College to sponsor a teacher's training course in Pakistan for a student planning to become a teacher working with Bradford's Asian communities.

calls to Britain's wealthy South Asians have with one exception gone largely unanswered. A group of South Asians in Bradford have set up the Pukaar Foundation and although its initial fundraising efforts have been disappointing a second Pukaar Foundation looks set to be launched later this year in the Luton/Bedford area.

However the South Asian Development Partnership claims a much higher success rate. Formed in 1989 'to encourage South Asians to participate in the economic development of the UK', international director Deepak Mahtani estimates at least 20 new trusts have been set up by wealthy UK South Asians as a result of SADP's work.

Table 3

Britain's wealthiest Asians

The 24 wealthiest Asians in Britain, 1999
(source for wealth figures and ranking: *Eastern Eye, Britain's Richest Asian 200, 1999* [1998 figures in brackets])

1. Srichand and Gopi Hinduja
£1,300 million (£1,200 million)
Foundation and charity links: the Hinduja Foundation

Not only are the Hinduja brothers the wealthiest Asians in Britain, they are also the eighth wealthiest Britons, according to *The Sunday Times Rich List 1999*. Despite the pair's dislike of publicity, they are well known for their philanthropy both in Britain and world-wide through their network of Hinduja Foundations. However the last two years have brought mixed fortunes. Despite their wealth continuing to grow (they overtook the Mittals to rise to the top spot in the *Eastern Eye* listing), with an estimated rise in their worth from £1,100 million in 1996 to £1,300 million by 1999, the failure of two ventures in both business and philanthropy is likely to have dented morale.

Plans by a group of Asian businessmen to establish a UK-Asian bank, led by SP Hinduja, were dealt a mortal blow when Midland, part of HSBC investment bank, finally pulled out of the deal. On the philanthropy side the Hindujas' ambitious £100 million Concordia project failed to secure the necessary backing from the Millennium Board. The scheme involved establishing a multicultural high-technology park in Peterborough in a collaboration between the Hindujas, the Hinduja Foundation and donations from the Asian community. However, whilst it is unlikely to be revived in its former incarnation, the Hindujas insist that Concordia may still happen and are reportedly trying to negotiate through a London-based partner. The Hinduja brothers have recently been in the limelight following the row over their offer to underwrite the threatened Spirit Zone at the Millennium Dome, reportedly at a cost of £6 million. Their desire for an area celebrating 'multi-faith harmony' annoyed Church leaders who felt the celebration of 2,000 years of Christianity was being undermined by devout Hindu businessmen. Despite this third establishment snub, the pair are remarkable philanthropists, estimated to give between £45 million and £60 million to charity each year. The UK-based Hinduja Foundation donates approximately £100,000 a year.

2. Lakshmi & Usha Mittal
£1,200 million (£2,000 million)
Foundation and charity links: none identified

The Mittals have slipped into second place in the *Eastern Eye* listing following a disappointing year business-wise, which saw the share price in their steel business dip dramatically. Following the flotation of the Ispat steel empire, the Mittals are continuing an impressive programme of expansion. Despite the Mittals' wealth and reported generosity there is little evidence of philanthropy from this intensely private pair.

3. Subhash Chandra
£450 million (£450 million)
Foundation and charity links: none identified

Chandra is the owner of Zee TV, the UK Asian TV channel, as well as numerous other ventures into amusement parks, tube manufacturing and cosmetics. However, there is no information available on any philanthropic involvement by Chandra, who avowedly enjoys his anonymity.

4. Lord Paul
£325 million (£500 million)
Foundation and charity links: The Ambika Paul Foundation

Unusually amongst those listed here, Lord Paul is perhaps best known for his philanthropy, making headlines with his £1 million grant to London Zoo in 1995. However, recently Swraj Paul was ennobled by the new Labour government and is one of a minority of wealthy Asian businessmen who is publicly in favour of Labour. He is now said to have taken a back seat from his Caparo steel business, which had a difficult time in 1998, spending his time on the Government benches in the House of Lords and on his philanthropy. The Ambika Paul Foundation is named after his young daughter, who died of leukaemia in 1968.

5. Felix Grovit
£300 million (£300 million)
Foundation and charity links: none identified

Like many of his contemporaries in this listing Grovit eschews publicity and as a result there is no information available about philanthropic activity. A financier who established the Chequepoint foreign exchange chain, he was also behind the failed project to launch a rival to London's Evening Standard

41

newspaper at the end of the 1980s. Unlike Grovit's other business ventures the London News did not take off.

=6. Tom Singh
£200 million (£150 million)
Foundation and charity links: none identified

Singh's fashion retail business is said to hold 2.5 per cent of the women's wear market, though he has been reluctant to launch a possible flotation of his New Look company. Inspite of earlier setbacks and record sales in 1997 Singh looks destined to get a decent price for New Look in a flotation. However, as yet he appears not to have invested such energy in philanthropy.

=6. Jasminder Singh & family
£200 million (£150 million)
Foundation and charity links: none identified

Said to be a modest man, Jasminder Singh has virtually all the family's wealth tied up in his Edwardian hotel chain. He attributes his success to his staff at Edwardian, but it is not known whether this selflessness extends to any philanthropic endeavour.

=8. Manubhai Madhvani & family
£150 million (£150 million)
Foundation and charity links: British-Asian Ugandan Trust

Manubhai Madhvani is regarded as one of the leaders of the Ugandan Asian community in Britain, although his family has recently returned to Uganda following a request from the present Ugandan regime for their help in rebuilding the Ugandan economy. Madhvani describes his hobbies as travelling, photography and social work, and is said to be anonymously involved in many charities. He publicly took the helm of the British-Asian Ugandan Trust, which was set up to organise the celebrations to mark the 25th anniversary of Idi Amin's expulsion of 50,000 Asians from Uganda. Celebratory events included an address by the Ugandan president Yoweri Museveni at the charity-funded Swaminaryan Mandir in autumn 1997, a thanksgiving service at Westminster Abbey, a monument at Stanstead airport and a banquet. He is said to believe strongly in the need to eliminate cultural and political boundaries dividing British and Asian communities, feeling that unless the Asian community is completely integrated it may suffer the same fate that befell it in Uganda.

=9. Sir Anwar Pervez & family
£120 million (£120 million)
Foundation and charity links: The Bestway Foundation & other charities

Recently knighted, Anwar Pervez' Bestway cash-and-carry business is now worth around £180 million and Pervez' family owns 60 per cent of the shares. Originally from Pakistan where he used to walk eight miles to school each day, Anwar Pervez is proud of his meritocratic rags-to-riches story, stating: 'We were Thatcherites before Margaret Thatcher'. The foundation he established in his company's name distributes around £160,000 per year. In addition he is a benefactor of Age Concern and the Duke of Edinburgh's Award Scheme. He was knighted for his services to charity and the food industry.

=9 Gulu Lalvani
£120 million (£60 million)
Foundation and charity links: Leprosy Mission

Lalvani hit the headlines in 1997 when he escorted Princess Diana from a night-club, although it was insisted that the meeting had occurred because of his making a large donation to the Leprosy Mission. Founder of the Binatone electronics group, now the largest privately owned consumer electronics company in Britain, Lalvani helped Alan Sugar set up in business in 1966 and until 1998 held a 9 per cent stake in Amstrad.

11. Vijay and Bhikku Patel
£113 million (£25 million)
Foundation and charity links: none identified

The Patel brothers are at the head of Britain's pharmaceutical business. They run Waymade, an Essex-based pharmaceutical wholesale company which is often cited as one of Britain's fastest growing businesses. There is no evidence of charitable activity.

=12. Ratilal Chandaria
£100 million (£100 million)
Foundation and charity links: The Chandaria Foundation

Another reticent member of this ranking, East African Chandaria and his two brothers control Comcraft, an industrial group dealing in steel, chemicals and plastic across 40 countries. In 1967, Chandaria established the Chandaria Foundation, which currently makes grants totalling just £3,000 a year.

=12. Sonu Shivdasani
£100 million (£100 million)
Foundation and charity links: The Inlaks Foundation

Sonu replaces his mother Lakshmi Shivdasani in Eastern Eye's listing for 1997, despite her place as the matriarch in a low-profile family which is however well known for its philanthropy. The family business which has interests in resorts and finance extends far afield from India and Nigeria to France and Switzerland. Sonu is said to be the driving force in the family business. The foundation was set up in 1982 and annual grants total around £200,000, including scholarships, projects, and donations. It is registered in Liechtenstein.

=12. Tahir Mohsan and family
£100 million (£50 million)
Foundation and charity links: None identified

=12. Rasiklal Thakrar and family
£100 million (£13 million)
Foundation and charity links: None identified

16. Mike Jatania
£90 million (£12 million)
Foundation and charity links: None identified

17. Nat Puri
£85 million (£85 million)
Foundation and charity links: The Puri Foundation

Maths graduate Nat Puri came to Britain from India in 1966. Despite a fall in profits of his main holding company Melton Medes in 1997, he is still valued by *Eastern Eye* at £85 million. He is also the founder and benefactor of the Puri Foundation which was established in 1988. Its assets were valued at £1.9 million in 1996.

18. Humayun Mughal
£72 million (£45 million)
Foundation and charity links: None identified

19. Rashmi Thakrar
£70 million (£30 million)
Foundation and charity links: Tilda Foundation

The 'rice king' of Britain has seen profits rise steadily in his Tilda company in recent years. The eponymous Tilda Foundation currently donates approximately £38,000 a year and maintains close ties with Thakrar's company.

20. James Caan
£61 million (£3.4 million)
Foundation and charity links: None identified

=21. Lord & Apurv Bagri
£60 million (£80 million)
Foundation and charity links: The Bagri Foundation
Lord Bagri, founder of the Bagri Foundation, chairs the London Metal Exchange. Wishing to keep out of the charity public's eye, Bagri states modestly that he 'does not wish to see himself as a philanthropist since he feels strongly that he is fortunate to be in such a position.'

=21 Iqbal Ahmed
£60 million (new entry)
Foundation and charity links: None identified

=21. Shami Ahmed
£60 million (£60 million)
Foundation and charity links: none identified

Founder of the Manchester-based Joe Bloggs fashion chain, Ahmed is not frightened of publicity, formerly presenting Dosh, a Channel 4 guide to making money. A member of the government's welfare-to-work task force he also has property interests but is not known for charitable work.

=21. Gurchait & Gurnaik Chima
£50 million (£50 million)
Foundation and charity links: none identified

The two brothers own 100 per cent of the shares in this West Yorkshire-based ladies fashionwear business. Nothing is known about any charitable involvement.

25. Rajan Kumar
£50 million (£50 million)
Foundation and charity links: none identified

A new entry to the Eastern Eye listing, little is known about Kumar and nothing about any charitable giving,. The successful Rajan Group is another Manchester-based fashion group.

Others with known charity links:

=26. Gulam Noon
£40 million (£25 million)
Foundation and charity links: The Noon Foundation

=90 Damodar Chanrai
£10 million (£10 million)
Foundation and charity links: The Chanrai Foundation

It appears that the family glass, textile and property company provides the financial basis for the Chanrai Foundation, thought to fund Asian charities. As it is not a UK-registered charity there is no information available and it is probably based overseas.

The UK South Asian voluntary sector and the next millennium

Issues for funders, charities and policy makers

Whether or not the South Asian voluntary sector has a bright future will depend on whether it can build its own structures. As the general funding squeeze makes it likely that only the leaner and fitter voluntary organisations will survive, there is an acute need for South Asian voluntary organisations to be given access to the numerous fundraising and development skills which the mainstream voluntary sector has spent the last two decades fine tuning. At present, South Asian groups are not plugged into any significant networks through which they are likely to come across funders. Lack of experience and information on funding sources means that fundraising is largely ineffective or targeted inappropriately. Charitable funders must start to address the issues which so far have apparently eluded the vast majority. Clearly, as has been demonstrated on numerous occasions, a 'colour-blind' approach to charitable funding will result in the black and minority ethnic community voluntary sector encountering prejudice in the raising of funds. Recent estimates suggest that for this sector to receive its full share – as black and minority ethnic communities comprise 6 per cent of the total UK population – it should be collecting approximately £780 million of total charitable income (*Dimensions of the Voluntary Sector*, 1998). The real figures, whilst difficult to estimate accurately, fall far short of this figure, perhaps in the region of £300 to £400 million. Therefore funders need to address this shortfall urgently. Whilst the figures available on the funding to the black voluntary sector only provide a partial picture it is clear that what is given is woefully inadequate. In 1997/98 the black charity Sia distributed £2 million of Single Renovation Budget (SRB) funding to black groups, whilst the Home Office's Voluntary and Community Unit distributed £408,000 to minority community groups. Although the National Lottery Charities Board allocated £27.6 million to projects specifically targeted at minority communities, approximately 9 per cent of total funds distributed, none of the other lottery distributors can produce an ethnic breakdown of grants awarded. An approximate guesstimate of local authority grant aid indicates a total of just £18 million annually, based on the £8 million distributed to black groups by London local authorities. Whilst the figures presented here appear small, it is clear that the black and minority community voluntary sector must be in receipt of more income if only evidenced by their continued existence. What is clear is the lack of ethnic monitoring of grant aid across the whole spectrum of funders – from local government to charitable trusts.

Despite the attempts of some UK mainstream charities to re-target their policies and services towards South Asian communities and other black and minority ethnic communities, there is still more work to be done. Sadly, it seems that only the realisation that the 'South Asian market' is ripe for picking will provide the motivation for mainstream charities to re-focus their work. At the same time they must realise that they will only succeed in tapping this market if they genuinely manage to meet the needs of the members of all Britain's South Asian communities and are able to make their approach culturally and ethnically acceptable to those communities. For they are competing with a vibrant, if undeveloped, sector of voluntary and community organisations, which can only get stronger as both their own philanthropy gains ground and their techniques of accessing funds improve.

It is arguable that through neglect the mainstream voluntary sector has forfeited its right to represent the needs of black and minority communities. Perhaps the limited funding available should therefore be directed towards those black and minority community voluntary organisations already meeting the needs of their communities.

The new frontier of voluntary activity

The South Asian voluntary sector is itself in a state of increased transition. Britain's South Asian communities are facing new challenges unknown to the first generation of immigrants, including drug abuse, HIV, AIDS, and the high suicide rates amongst young women. The sector is adapting to meet these needs, with a new generation of South Asian voluntary organisations involved in the provision of services within the community, while older, more established organisations have tended to prioritise the maintenance of cultural, traditional and religious identities. However, the flexibility of the South Asian voluntary sector means that it is better positioned than the mainstream voluntary sector to meet these new needs.

However, the local and informal nature of many of the voluntary organisations serving South Asian and other black and minority ethnic communities is also its weakness. Constraints imposed by a lack of resources mean that only a small number of these groups advocate, lobby, litigate, monitor government performance, conduct multi-purpose comprehensive programmes, or engage in public policy issues. It is in these areas that the South Asian voluntary sector must find its voice. If they can, they will rightly challenge the funding monopoly currently held by Britain's mainstream voluntary sector. If they can't, charitable funders may continue to ignore the opportunity to recognise what is an integral part of British society at the beginning of a new millennium.

For the next millennium

At the time of publication (summer 1999), it appears that a breakthrough in the funding of black and minority community groups may at last have been made with the birth of a foundation created and owned by Britain's ethnic minority communities. The Ethnic Minority Foundation aims to finally rid the ethnic minority voluntary sector from restricted access to charitable funds. It estimates that despite constituting 6 per cent of the population Britain's ethnic minority communities receive less than 2 per cent of voluntary funding from all sources. This ambitious project, led by Trevor Phillips, Sir Herman Ousley, Usha Prashar and Amir Bhatia, aims to create a £100 million endowment over the next ten years. The foundation aims to raise the endowment by enrolling 100,000 ethnic minority professionals. Each will be asked to make three commitments: to act as trustees, advisory committee members, professional advisers and policy makers; to volunteer to mentor one ethnic minority student on a one-to-one basis; and to donate £100 a year for ten years.

The foundation will then provide crucial long-term core funding to ethnic minority voluntary sector organisations, as well as short-term project funding and other grant initiatives.

If successful the foundation will provide a huge boost to the flagging funding scene in which the ethnic minority voluntary sector is fighting to stay afloat. If it can build an endowment which matches or even exceeds the projected figures, the Ethnic Minority Foundation will not only be the biggest single funder of the ethnic minority voluntary sector but one of the 20 biggest charitable funders in the UK. It will not only provide funds but a powerful voice able to lobby on behalf of all ethnic minority voluntary sector organisations.

Section Two

■■■■■■■■■■■■■■■■■■■■■■■■■■■■■■■■■■■■■

Grant-making trusts with connections to the South Asian voluntary sector

Introduction

Grant-making trusts are an invaluable source of funding to voluntary organisations in the UK. Research commissioned by the Charities Aid Foundation puts their estimated total grant-making expenditure at virtually £2 billion (*Dimensions of the Voluntary Sector, 1997*). The range of trusts in terms of grant-making interest, professional application and size is huge: the top 300 grant-making trusts together award grants in excess of £1.1 billion a year, in amounts ranging from £50 to in excess of £1 million. Just as valuable, however, are the many thousands of small local trusts, which, whilst they may each make grants totalling less than £1,000 a year, often have a far greater commitment to the area in which they operate.

The greatest strength of grant-making trusts has always lain in their independence and their relative lack of public accountability which gives them the ability to strike new ground. Popularly known in the 1970s and 1980s as 'pump primers', in that they were prepared to provide start-up funding to new projects, trusts have been marked by their willingness to lend support to causes which fall between the main stools of statutory funding programmes. In their strength however lies their inherent weakness. Whilst for the handful of more progressive trusts the above is undoubtedly true, for the vast majority of the estimated 9,000 UK trusts in operation (*Dimensions of the Voluntary Sector, 1997*), there is not even lip service paid to notions of equality of opportunity in grant-making practice. The gravity of the situation becomes apparent when the top 300 trusts are scrutinised for their willingness to provide general information on procedures, policy and practice. Figures based on information provided by the top 300 trusts listed in *A Guide to the Major Trusts, Volume 1, 1997/98* give little heart to those urging trusts to develop not just their own accountability, but positive practices towards disadvantaged groups. As co-editor Susan Forrester states: 'It is a sombre fact that fewer than half of the top 100 grant-making trusts – all giving over £1 million a year – publish annual reports of any kind.' (see Table 4). The situation is actually worse in terms of trusts producing even the most basic guidelines for applicants. 'Only a quarter of all trusts listed in this guide (all giving over £200,000 a year)', says Forrester, 'produce policy and applicants' guidelines.' (see Table 5)

Table 4

Information provided to applicants by the major-grant-making trusts

Trusts publishing annual reports* %

Trusts giving £1 million +	47%
All 300 major trusts	28%

* Reports available for public circulation (not only to fulfil Charity Commission requirements for a narrative report under the Charities Act 1993)

Source: *Trust Monitor, 1997*

Table 5

Trusts providing guidelines for applicants	1997/98	1995/96
Trusts giving £1 million +	38%	27%
All 300 major trusts	24%	18%

Source: *Trust Monitor, 1997*

The implications for positive policies on funding of black organisations are alarming. As far back as 1992, Mark Lattimer, author of *Funding Black Groups*, argued that the colour-blind 'we are open to all' approach, adopted by most grant-making trusts, was woefully inadequate. Whilst funders apparently acknowledged disadvantages experienced by minority community groups in obtaining charitable funding, few trusts were prepared to do anything concrete to combat it. 'There was overwhelming support for a "colour blind" approach, with over 80 per cent of funders believing that ethnic minority status should be disregarded when considering applications.' (*Funding Black Groups*, 1992)

An end to colour blindness?

The consequence of such a policy (or lack of it) with regard to funding black voluntary organisations is that they receive less rather than equal funding from trusts. As Lattimer points out: 'over half the black groups in the survey had never received more than £1,000 in total in charitable grant aid'. *Funding Black Groups* included a paltry list of 22 grant-making trusts which had either specific policies towards or were known to be major funders of minority community organisations. Seven years on, this list has expanded to include 43 of the top 300 grant-making trusts, but this is still a shocking indictment of the trust world's reactivity not just to a multi-cultural voluntary sector, but to multi-cultural Britain.

The Confederation of Indian Organisations' *Directory of Asian Voluntary Organisations 1994/95* lists 22 charitable trusts deemed useful to potential applicants. None of these are specifically oriented towards South Asian or minority community groups, although virtually all have positive policies towards their support.

Emerging South Asian trusts

There is however evidence that, akin to the now established Jewish voluntary sector, UK South Asians are doing it for themselves. Section Two lists trusts with a South Asian connection, the large majority of which have been set up in the 1990s. A significant number of them have not appeared in any trust listing before. Together they give around £15 million a year, but there is some evidence that this is the tip of a hitherto untouched iceberg.

At the time of publication plans for a new £100 million foundation had been revealed. The Ethnic Minority Foundation aims to create a endowment of £100 million over the next ten years to provide grants to organisations in the 'ethnic minority voluntary sector'. In the wake of a clear refusal of the majority of the UK's grant-making trusts to positively address the needs of Britain's black and minority community voluntary sector, the Ethnic Minority Foundation aims to redress this imbalance.

Special points about the trust listing

The list is inevitably selective and we make our apologies to trusts which have been inadvertently omitted from the list. In addition, inclusion in the listing should not be taken to automatically imply a static grants policy.

The details given below contain only the briefest outline of the trust's full grant-making policy. Before applying to any of these trusts full details of grant-making policy and practice should ideally be sought to ensure a greater chance of success. As will be seen from the cursory details contained below, the trusts' interest in funding minority community organisations varies immensely, ranging from funding for refugee welfare and racial equality projects to support for multi-cultural education and the developing world.

Applicants should note that inclusion in the listing does not necessarily mean specific funding support is available for South Asian voluntary organisations, but the list includes trusts which either have a stated or apparent connection to Britain's South Asian communities. It must not be assumed that trusts which do not appear in this listing will not support minority community groups, simply that any grants to these organisations are qualified within a different area of support, or not specified.

Warning to applicants!

The trusts should be approached with extreme care! For whilst every effort has been made to ensure accuracy of published information, inclusion of a trust does not necessarily imply its willingness to be listed. Each trust has been sent a copy of their entry in this listing and where they have responded their comments have been duly noted. We ask our readers to exercise great care when making applications to these trusts. Nothing makes our task harder or a grant-making trust's life more frustrating than when fundraisers send indiscriminate mailings to any trust which happens to take their fancy. This is the first attempt to compile a listing of trusts connected to Britain's South Asian communities and has been a large and difficult task. In addition to the many trusts listed below for whom there was inadequate information available on public file at the Charity Commission, there were dozens more on whom there was no available information at all. It was therefore not possible to include many trusts who are quite possibly doing very good work within Britain's South Asian communities and elsewhere.

However, the research for this book has been done as fully and carefully as was possible. We are very grateful to the many trust officers, trustees and others who have helped us in this.

Inevitably some of the information contained in this listing is incomplete or will have become out-of-date. If any reader comes across omissions or errors whilst reading this listing, please let us know so they can be rectified in future editions. A message to the London Office Research Department of the Directory of Social Change (020 7209 4422 or info@dsc.org.uk) would be much appreciated.

We wish you all the best in your fundraising.

New telephone codes

Please note that from 22 April 2000, telephone numbers will officially change in the following areas:

Cardiff	Portsmouth
Coventry	Southampton
London	Northern Ireland

Where applicable, new numbers are given in brackets. In the changeover period from June 1999 to Autumn 2000, either number can be used.

Top 15 trusts from the following list by grant total

Aga Khan Foundation: £6,735,000 (1995)
Muslim Aid: £1,909,889 (1998)
The Al-Khoei Benevolent Foundation: £1,345,000
Mercury Phoenix Trust: £893,000 (1996)
Sri Satya Sai (UK) Trust: £302,000 (1996)
Christmas Cracker Trust: £295,000 (1996)
Muslim Hands: £254,000 (1995)
Alternative for India Development: (AID) £238,000 (1999)
Inlaks Foundation (UK): £220,000 (1996)
The Human Relief Foundation: £207,000 (1996)
Bestway Foundation: £164,000 (1996)
Islamic Relief Agency: £140,000 (1998)
Altajir Trust (Altajir World of Islam Trust): £134,000 (1995)
International Network for the Development of India in Action: £110,000 (1998)
The Hinduja Foundation: £104,000 (1995)

The Trusts

Action for the Development of India

Grant total: Not available
Work: General
Beneficial area: West Midlands and India
Charity Commission number: 1041662
There is little information currently available on this relatively new trust and unfortunately it has not been possible to glean any more information from the correspondent. Its file at the Charity Commission shows it was established in

1994, but there are no accounts or information on the trust's aims and activities, although it looks likely to be a grant-maker.
Trustees: Not available.
Correspondent: Mr Balwant Rai Bharti, General Secretary, 33 Rosemary Crescent West, Goldthorn Park, Wolverhampton WV4 5AP. Tel: 01902 334475.

Fizza Adamjee Trust

Grant total: £9,000 (1993)
Work: Education
Beneficial area: UK and East Africa
Charity Commission number: 201517
Although the trust was first registered over 30 years ago, there is only basic information available on public file at the Charity Commission. The last set of accounts available from the Charity Commission was for 1993 and showed an income of £12,000 and a grant total of £9,000. Despite numerous contacts made with the correspondent it was not possible to ascertain precisely what the trust has done since 1993, although it appears to provide small educational grants.
Application details: in writing to the correspondent.
Trustees: Abdulla Mohamedali; Ali Bhai Karimjee; Hamza Akberali Alavi.
Correspondent: Mrs Eileen Gray, 21 Whitefriars Street, London EC4Y 8JJ. Tel: 0171 583 3768 (020 7583 3768), e-mail: eileengray@dial.pipex.com

Aga Khan Foundation

Grant total: £6,735,000 (1995)
Work: Education, health and rural development overseas
Beneficial area: Numerous countries including India, Pakistan, Bangladesh and the UK
Charity Commission number: 266518
The foundation was established in 1967 by His Highness the Aga Khan in the belief that everyone should have the opportunity to find the dignity that comes with self-reliance. It is currently pursuing these objectives by helping communities in Bangladesh, Canada, India, Kenya, Pakistan, Tajikistan, Tanzania, Uganda, the UK and the USA. It is an institution of the Ismaili branch of Islam and part of a network of foundations worldwide called the Aga Khan Development Network. All administration costs are paid by the Aga Khan himself and so all income is directly available for grants.

Projects are identified by local communities. Grants are made to reputable, large or small, organisations with demonstrated leadership and management capacity, whose activities have improved the quality of life of the people.

The foundation concentrates on innovative, cost-effective and able-to-be-replicated projects and is focusing on the following areas:

- child development and effective education for the future, through improving the quality of formal education and early childhood education;
- family health and nutrition, through community-oriented health development;
- rural development, through income generation and management of renewable resources;
- increasing local human resources through the development of skills and training opportunities and professional and technical exchanges between countries and institutions.

Applications are welcome at any time during the year, but please note that grants are not normally made for capital development, endowment, research, expeditions, project placements overseas, conferences, meetings and core administration costs.

Trustees: His Highness the Aga Khan, Chair; Prince Amyn Aga Khan; Maitre Andre Ardoin; Guillaume de Spoelberch.

Correspondent: Mr Aly-Raza Nazerali, 3 Cromwell Gardens, London SW7 2HB. Tel: 0171 591 6800 (020 7591 6800).

The Al-Khoei Benevolent Foundation

Grant total: £1,345,000 (but see below)
Work: Islam-related relief and education
Beneficial area: UK and overseas
Charity Commission number: 802000

Established in 1989, the foundation currently has assets amounting to over £6 million. Its aims are to advance the Islamic religion by providing and maintaining mosques and religious centres, and teaching young people of the Islamic community the practices and doctrines of Islam.

However, most of the trust's expenditure, which totalled £1.4 million in 1995, is allocated directly to the Al-Khoei school, magazine and mosque. It appears that most of the trust's income is also derived from these areas.

In response to a request for further information, the correspondent states that the foundation is also involved in: 'inter-faith, inter-community dialogue, working at local, regional and international level in other related spheres, notably the advancement of human rights and development, especially in educating those who may not have access to such needs'. The foundation supports English teaching projects for refugee children, applications for asylum by refugees and women in desperate circumstances.

Trustees: S M A Shahrestani; S A M Khoei; M A Najafi; Y A Nafsi; K A H Mohammed.

Correspondent: Nadeem Kazmi, c/o Merali, Scottish Provident House, 76–80 College Road, Harrow, Middlesex HA1 1BX. Tel: 0171 372 4049 (020 7372 4049).

Mohamed Ali Foundation

Grant total: £1,000 (1996)
Work: Islamic education and history
Beneficial area: UK and overseas
Charity Commission number: 279253

Established in 1979, with princesses as trustees, the foundation is not as large as one might first expect, with assets standing at £50,000 in 1996.

The foundation was established to advance public awareness in the history of the Islamic world, Egypt and the Mohamed Ali family. However, it can also support more general causes.

Although in 1996 the foundation's total charitable grants had halved compared with previous years to just £1,000, its income and asset base had both increased slightly.

Trustees: Princess Abbas Hilmi; Princess Medhia Hilmi; Princess Sabiha Hilmi.

Correspondent: Princess Medhia Hilmi, 20a Pembridge Villas, London W11 2SU. Tel: 0171 229 5999 (020 7229 5999).

Altajir Trust (Altajir World of Islam Trust)

Grant total: £134,000 (1995)
Work: General and education
Beneficial area: UK, Arab or Islamic states
Charity Commission number: 284116

Since its registration in 1982 the trust has not increased its size in any notable way, with its assets remaining at just under £40,000. With an average annual income of around £160,000, the trust tends to give away most of this each year, predominantly helping students. In 1995 awards totalling £134,000 were made.

Trustees: Dr Roger Williams; Alan Jones; Peter Tripp; H E Mohammed Al Tajir.

Correspondent: A C Duncan, 33 Thurloe Place, London SW7 2HQ. Tel: 0171 581 3522 (020 7 581 3522), Fax: 0171 584 1977 (020 7584 1977).

Alternative for India Development (AID)

Grant total: £238,000 (1999)
Work: General
Beneficial area: India
Charity Commission number: 297944

This trust was first registered at the Charity Commission in 1987, although it was originally founded five years earlier by young people in India and the UK.

AID run a variety of training programmes, including technical, vocational and health training for the rural poor, and literacy centres. By providing adult education for women it seeks to liberate them from prostitution, the child marriage system, untouchability and caste distinctions. Its environmental projects aim to prevent deforestation and encourage the planting of new trees. The trust also encourages people from India who are settled abroad to involve themselves in its development activities, and provides information to Europeans about rural life in India.

There are plans to provide non-formal skills training for tribal women and organise networking between non-government organisations in India and development organisations in the UK. The charity also hopes to sell handicraft items produced by rural artisans in India.

The accounts on file at the Charity Commission show a steady income – rising to £90,000 in 1997 – whilst expenditure amounted to £67,000 in the same year. Unfortunately there are no details as to which organisations received grant-aid. In 1998 it is known grants had risen substantially, totalling £238,000, but it is thought that the vast bulk of this was directed towards the trust's own projects with only a very small amount available for distribution to other organisations.

Trustees: B R Sohpal; R Kumar; H Kattaria; G D Rattu.

Correspondent: B R Sohpal, Chair, 84 Aylesford Road, Handsworth, Birmingham B21 8DW. Tel: 0121 554 5854.

Ancient India and Iran Trust (AIIT)

Grant total: £25,000 (1996) but see below
Work: Education in Indo-Iranian language, history and culture
Beneficial area: UK and South Asia
Charity Commission number: 276295

Set up in 1978, the trust has a secure financial base with investments valued at around £840,000 in 1996/97, which produce a steady income. Income and expenditure are reasonably similar, totalling £136,000 and £128,000 respectively in 1996/97.

The correspondent states that the trustees' policy is: 'first to maintain the house (Brooklands House in Cambridge), and to maintain and catalogue its library, which is open daily for scholars and members of the public; second to support conferences, organise seminars and lectures, promote relevant publications, and support a Visiting Professorship from India; and third, as and when funds are available, to make small grants in aid of research'.

In 1996/97 direct charitable expenditure included: Brooklands House maintenance (£11,000), library and cataloguing (£17,000); publishing (£4,600). However, the correspondent states that the trust is not currently in a position to make grants.

The trust is also linked to the J Van Lohuizen Bequest, which has a further balance of £217,000.

Trustees: Sir Harold Walter Bailey; James Harle; Neil Kreitman; Sir Nicholas Barrington; Nicholas Sims-Williams; Dr Giles Tillotson.
Correspondent: Dr F R Allchin, Chair, Brooklands House, 23 Brooklands Avenue, Cambridge CB2 2BG. Tel: 01223 356841.

Jehangir Manek Anklesaria Charitable Trust

Grant total: £35,000 (1998)
Work: Hospitals
Beneficial area: UK and overseas
Charity Commission number: 275586
This trust was set up in 1978 in order to make grants to hospitals or similar institutions for the purchase of heart, kidney or lung machines, or appliances to be used for charitable purposes.

With assets in excess of £100,000 the trust operates a biennial grants round, providing institutions with the medical equipment indicated above in grants of approximately £5,000 each. However, the application procedure is tight. As stipulated in the will of the settler the trust must advertise in the *British Medical Journal* and does not seek publicity for its work elsewhere. The last grant round which totalled £35,000 was made in 1998 and the next grants will not be available until the year 2000.
Trustees: Midland Bank Trust Company.
Correspondent: Mr Derek Eyles, Trust Controller, Midland Bank Trust Co Ltd, Cumberland House, 15-17 Cumberland Place, Southampton, Hampshire SO15 2UY. Tel: 01703 531385 (023 80531385), Fax: 01703 531341 (023 80531341).

Arihant Charitable Trust

Grant total: £11,000 (1996)
Work: General
Beneficial area: UK
Charity Commission number: 1007733
Since its inception in 1992 this relatively small trust has grown steadily. It now has assets amounting to £100,000, and gives out grants of around £10,000 each year.

The religious background of the trustees is that of the Jains, although the trust's grant policy does not seem bound in any particular direction. In 1995 the trust made numerous small grants – ranging from £2,500 to just £25 – to a variety of development, religious and health-related organisations, including: Jain Samaj MCR (£2,500); Institute of Jainology (£1,000); Oxfam Rwanda (£250); Guy's Hospital (£150); Salvation Army (£25).
Trustees: Hasmukh Mehta; Supendra Mehta; Mayur Mehta; Dinesh Mehta.
Correspondent: Mayur Vrajlal Mehta, Kippold Ltd, Cheetwood House, Cheetwood Road, Cheetham, Manchester M8 1LH. Tel: 0161 792 4040.

Asha Foundation

Grant total: Not available, but see below
Work: General
Beneficial area: UK and overseas (particularly India)
Charity Commission number: 1058320

Set up in 1996, the foundation claims its main mission is to 'bridge religions, nationalities, and cultures'. It plans to do this through working with other charities, companies, community groups and individuals.

The foundation's first major collaboration was in 1997 when it was one of the five charities involved in the Channel 5 'Give 5' appeal. The funds received by the Asha Foundation from this appeal were used to support projects helping India's street children.

Due to the short period of time that the foundation has been running, there is currently very little information available, although latterly it has been preoccupied with a multi-million pound project to build a multi-faith centre in the London Borough of Harrow. Targeting Britain's minority ethnic communities, the trust is currently negotiating match funding for a £10 million Millennium Commission grant.

Trustees: Annabelle Boal; Pesh Framjee; Genie Irani; Gareth Marr; Michael Norton; Ramesh Vala.
Correspondent: Mr Ramesh Vala, c/o Geoff Green Russell, Apollo House, 56 New Bond Street, London W1Y 05X. Tel: 0171 499 7020 (020 7499 7020).

Asha Trust

Grant total: about £2,000 a year
Work: General
Beneficial area: India and England
Charity Commission number: 1058568

This small trust is typical of a grant-maker set up by individuals within a local community. Established with the broad remit of providing assistance to people in need in both India and England, the trust makes small grants largely to needy individuals in the Calcutta area of India, which is where many of those involved with the trust originated. Small grant payments are made to individuals in India for a range of purposes, including cataract operations, as well as to small charities in India which are not able to find funding from elsewhere. All the trust's income is derived from local community fundraising and the local authority is yet to provide any funding for the trust's work, despite requests from the trust for a grant to fund a local community centre. In addition to its small grants the trust also runs language classes and provides travel assistance to elderly and young people.

The trust has a 10-strong board of trustees and has members across Europe and the sub-continent.

59

Trustees: Not available.
Correspondent: Mr Sukumar Mitra, 89 Winchester Avenue, Kingsbury, London NW9 9TA. Tel: 0181 204 9704 (020 8204 9704).

Bagri Foundation

Grant total: £46,000 (1997)
Work: General
Beneficial area: UK and overseas
Charity Commission number: 1000219

This foundation was set up by the Bagri family in 1990 with a large asset base which now stands at almost £2 million and appears to still be growing. Its last set of accounts record an income of £113,000 and charitable grants totalling £46,000, which was significantly down from the 1996 grant total of £97,000.

Unfortunately there is very little information as to what the foundation's grants policy is, other than that it is known that grants are awarded solely at the discretion of the trustees with no clear indication of any direction to awards, and who has received grants in the past. The correspondent was reluctant for even this limited entry to be included. This might be due to a reluctance from the founder Raj Bagri, one of the UK's richest Asian businessmen, to assume a higher public profile. *Eastern Eye* magazine, compilers of Britain's *Richest Asian 200*, value Bagri and his son Apurv at £60 million.
Trustees: Lord Bagri CBE; Hon Apurv Bagri; Lady Bagri; R J Gatehouse.
Correspondent: Lynn Stokes, Metdist Limited, 80 Cannon Street, London EC4N 6EJ. Tel: 0171 606 8321 (020 7606 8321); Fax: 0171 606 6650 (020 7606 6650).

Barakat Trust

Grant total: £51,000 (1993)
Work: Islamic art and architecture
Beneficial area: Islamic countries
Charity Commission number: 328664

Set up in 1987 for the study, promotion and understanding of Islamic art, architecture and archaeology, the trust primarily provides financial support to students and scholars of Islamic culture. Grants are also made through educational institutions and in support of exhibitions, conferences, conservation projects and publications.

Disappointingly, especially considering the depth of the trust's work, representatives for this trust were extremely reluctant for an entry to be included in this listing stating: 'although there are Islamic countries within Asia, the trust is primarily targeted towards Saudi Arabia and other Middle Eastern countries and it is considered that an entry in an [Asian] directory is the wrong focus for the trust. The trustees are also concerned about being inundated by inappropriate applications, thereby increasing the administration costs of the trust'.

Bearing the above in mind, grants have been made to the Royal College of Art, Oxford University and Crosswell Photographic Archive, all in 1993.

Unfortunately it was not possible to ascertain more up-to-date details of the trust's work.

Trustees: H A Alireza; T A Alireza; A E Alireza.

Correspondent: Messrs Lawrence Jones Solicitors, Sea Containers House, 20 Upper Ground, Blackfriars Bridge, London SE1 9LH. Tel: 0171 620 1311 (020 7620 1311).

Bestway Foundation

Grant total: £164,000 (1996)
Work: Education
Beneficial area: UK and overseas
Charity Commission number: 297178

Funded by the Bestway chain of food stores, the foundation was set up in 1987 to provide grants, endowments, scholarships and loans for educational purposes. The company which bears its name was established in 1976 by Sir Anwar Pervez, himself valued by *Eastern Eye* magazine at £120 million, and is now Britain's second largest cash-and-carry business.

In 1996 the foundation made numerous grants amounting to £164,000. Amounts ranged from just £35 to the Midland Bank Olympic Appeal, to a more substantial £40,000 awarded to Age Concern UK. Other grants included £16,000 to the Duke of Edinburgh's Award Scheme, £6,000 to the National Grocers Benevolent Fund and £1,000 to the Ilford Islamic Centre. It also appears that the foundation is prepared to make grants to individuals.

Application details: Apply in writing with a brief letter and an SAE. Telephone calls are discouraged.

Trustees: Abdul Bhatti; Adalat Choudhary; Hussein Sheikh; Zameer Choudrey; Mohammed Pervez; Sabiha Pervez; Zia Khan.

Correspondent: Ms D Taylor, Bestway Cash & Carry Ltd, Abbey Road, Park Royal, London NW10 7BW. Tel: 0181 453 1234 (020 8453 1234).

Chandaria Foundation

Grant total: £3,000 (1994)
Work: General
Beneficial area: UK and overseas
Charity Commission number: 252669

Although this Hindu-based foundation was set up over 30 years ago, there is surprisingly little information on public record. Its last set of accounts at the Charity Commission are for 1994, and show income to be just £100, whilst expenditure totalled just over £3,000 and assets stood at £4,200. In contrast to the trust's size, its founder Ratilal Chandaria is Britain's 12th richest Asian according to *Eastern Eye*'s Rich Listing and worth £100 million.

Grants in 1994 included £200 to Oxfam Rwanda Relief, £250 to Young Indian Vegetarians and £200 to the Swaminaryan Hindu Mission.

Trustees: Kapoor Chandaria, Ratilal Premchand Chandaria.

Correspondent: Ratilal Chandaria, 49 Queens Gardens, London W2 3AA. Tel: 0171 723 2323 (020 7723 2323), Fax: 0171 724 9297 (020 7724 9297), e-mail: csl@comcraft.com

Christmas Cracker Trust

Grant total: £295,000 (1996)
Work: Christianity and development
Beneficial area: UK and overseas
Charity Commission number: 802266

The Christmas Cracker Trust was set up in 1989 and has now raised over £1.5 million for people in need. It has done this through a number of innovative ideas which involve more than just donating cash.

The original project involved getting young people to set up restaurants over the Christmas period, formed on a principle of 'eat less, pay more'. Given help from the trust's central office, young people used empty buildings in high streets, and cooked their own food and sold it to the public. The trust's next idea was to set up radio stations over the festive period, seeking sponsorship and advertising, and charging for each record requested and played. This was based on the motto 'tune in, pay out'. Alongside this the trust have set up 'Crackerterias', selling tea, coffee and simple snacks to the public. As well as providing refreshments to customers, they also aim to educate people in the problems of the developing world, especially those directly linked to mass consumption by the West.

During 1994, the trust decided to expand its fundraising period from just Christmas to the whole year. The trust got involved with GMTV's 'Get up and give' appeal, the annual week-long fundraiser, donating the money raised to six charity organisations.

The money raised by the trust is given out in grants to various Christian development organisations around the world. In 1996, the charity had an income of £450,000, another increase on the previous year. This allowed for grants of nearly £300,000 to be made.

Trustees: Not available.

Correspondent: Mr Suneel Shivdasani, PO Box 43, Sutton, Surrey SM2 5WZ.

Dewan Iqbal Foundation

Grant total: Not known
Work: Relief of poverty, sickness, disability; advancement of education and self-sufficiency
Beneficial area: Bangladesh
Charity Commission number: 1038390

A small foundation set up essentially for the benefit of Bangladesh, its support is aimed principally at the relief of poverty, sickness, disability and the advancement of education and self-sufficiency.

The accounts on file at the Charity Commission for 1996 show income and expenditure on a level footing at around £3,500, although as expenditure appears to have been solely for administration purposes it is unknown to what extent grants are available from the foundation.

However, through information provided by the correspondent it appears that whilst not a large grant maker, the foundation is pursuing an innovative approach to development work providing micro-credit to villagers in Bangladesh. Under this system the foundation effectively provides small loans to villages, which have included both fishing and farming communities. The funds are available for a variety of purposes, including buying seeds to plant crops, and the strategy appears to have been very successful.

The foundation is run by the founder, Dewan Iqbal Choudhury, who is of Bangladeshi origin.

Trustees: D I Choudhury; M Choudhury; N I Choudhury.
Correspondent: Dewan Iqbal Choudhury, Chair, 34 Glenavon Road, Prenton, Merseyside L43 0RE. Tel: 0151 608 9353.

East West Children Trust

Grant total: Not available
Work: Children
Beneficial area: Sri Lanka
Charity Commission number: 1049368

Unfortunately the information contained on file at the Charity Commission is very limited, which is a shame as it is perhaps one of the only known trusts set up specifically to support people in Sri Lanka. The trust was set up in 1995 for the benefit of children in Sri Lanka and, although there is no available grant total, the correspondent emphasised that although it is an active grant-maker it is a small trust. Grants are typically made to projects helping orphans and other Sri Lankan children in need.

Trustees: Mr A Mohanadas; Mr S Kamal; Mr K Gengatharan.
Correspondent: Mr T Pasupathy, Chair, 26 Lapstone Gardens, Kenton, Harrow, Middlesex HA3 0ED. Tel: 0181 907 1677 (020 8907 1677).

Ethnic Minority Foundation

Grant total: See below
Work: Ethnic minorities
Beneficial area: UK
Charity Commission number: currently seeking registration

This new foundation is a major new initiative sponsored by four notable members of Britain's black and minority communities: Trevor Phillips, Sir Herman Ouseley, Amir Bhatia (founder of the Forbes Trust, listed below) and Usha Prashar. Recognising the acute funding needs of Britain's 'ethnic minority voluntary sector' the foundation is aiming to build a £100 million endowment over the next ten years. Planning to be a foundation 'created and owned by the ethnic minority communities' it will make grants of much needed long-term core funding (5 to 10 years), short-term project funding, as well as supporting other areas of ethnic minority community needs such as education, health and social welfare. Plans to build a £100 million endowment include enrolling the support of 100,000 ethnic minority professionals. They will be encouraged to give three commitments: support of the ethnic minority voluntary sector by acting as trustees, advisory committee members, professional advisors and policy makers; volunteering to mentor one ethnic minority student on a one-to-one basis; and a donation of £100 a year for ten years. Additional funding will also be sought from companies and trusts who will be asked to donate £100,000 a year for 10 years. The foundation is also hoping to secure a major one-off endowment donation from the government.

This is clearly an ambitious project, but reflects the firm will of influential members of Britain's black and minority communities to urgently address the funding crisis facing the ethnic minority voluntary sector in Britain. If successful in its ultimate aim of raising a £100 million endowment it will rank among the top 20 grant-making trusts in Britain.

Trustees: 15 trustees to be appointed – currently run by the four sponsors listed above.
Correspondent: Paul Butler, 9 Artillery Lane, London E1 7LP. Tel: 0171 247 6201 (020 7247 6201).

The Forbes Trust

Grant total: £31,000 (1998)
Work: General
Beneficial area: UK
Charity Commission number: 327358

Established in 1970 by the shareholders of one of the oldest trading houses in the UK, the trust aims to identify needs in the fields of education, health, the arts, and management, and to act as a catalyst in promoting and facilitating partnerships between foundations, charities, voluntary agencies, and other grant-making organisations. The main objectives of the trust are in the fields of:

- education – where the trust is particularly interested in innovative proposals designed to make education, at all levels, including the application of information technology, more effective and relevant to the needs of present and future society;
- health – where the trust aims to support initiatives directed towards the prevention of disease, and improved treatment in areas of special importance;
- the Arts – where the trust is hoping to encourage creative talent among students by promoting exhibitions and the production of new works;
- Project Management – where the trust will assist and collaborate with voluntary and charitable organisations in promoting training and good management in project finance, monitoring, and evaluation;
- income generation – where the trust will help create income generation schemes, particularly in Third World countries, by providing pump-priming funds for small-scale businesses.

The trust had assets of £190,000 in 1998, slightly down from 1996 when funds peaked at £244,000. Grants totalled £31,000 in 1998, down from £59,000 the year before, and were made to a range of different organisations some of which had also received grants in previous years. These included the Charities Evaluation Service (£6,000), Abantu (£5,000), Winchester College (£2,000), East London Partnership and Business in the Community (both £1,000). Unfortunately, particularly considering that Amir Bhatia is one of the leading and most high-profile South Asians working within the voluntary sector in Britain, Bhatia declined to be interviewed for this report. However at the time of writing there was news of an exciting new foundation set up with the involvement of Bhatia called the Ethnic Minority Foundation.

Trustees: Sir Hugh Casson; Sir Bryan Thwaites; Amir Bhatia; Mrs N Bhatia.
Correspondent: Amir Bhatia, Forbes House, 9 Artillery Lane, London E1 7LP. Tel: 0171 377 8484 (020 7377 8484).

Rajiv Gandhi (UK) Foundation

Grant total: about £2,000 a year
Work: Education (but see below)
Beneficial area: UK and India
Charity Commission number: 1032484

The foundation was set up in 1993 to advance education in Britain concerning India, its peoples, history, language and literature, institutions, culture, artistic and economic life, as well as to promote awareness of the environment. To date, in pursuit of these broad aims, although it was not possible to attain the exact size of disbursement, the trust has made small grants to UK students as well as visiting scholars from India, including those studying at Cambridge University and the London School of Economics.

Although the trust is currently small, with assets of just £18,000 in 1998, it does have big plans. The correspondent stated that there will be an incremental increase in activity by the trust in line with a planned but steadily increased income, and there are unspecified plans to also move into fields not connected to educational bursaries.

Trustees: Not available

Correspondent: Mr D K Singh, Hammond Suddards, 7 Devonshire Square, Cutlers Gardens, London EC2M 4ZH. Tel: 0171 655 1238 (020 7655 1238).

Gani Dewan Memorial Foundation

Grant total: £350 (1997)
Work: Education, poverty, sickness
Beneficial area: Bangladesh
Charity Commission number: 1010151

This is a very small foundation set up to help the people of Bangladesh, with a focus upon the education of young people under the age of 25. However, the foundation also cites the need to support those in need as a result of sickness, poverty and distress.

Finances appear to be limited, with the 1997 accounts on file at the Charity Commission showing an income of just £800, grants of just £350, and shrinking assets of £300.

Trustees: Not available.

Correspondent: D M Islam, 41 Ivatt Way, Tottenham, London N17 6PF. Tel: 0181 888 3952 (020 8888 3952).

Gurunanak

Grant total: £30,000 (1998)
Work: General
Beneficial area: Worldwide, but particularly the Preston/Manchester area in the UK
Charity Commission number: 1017903

This is a small Sikh-oriented organisation for the benefit of Sikhs in general, but set up in particular to advance the Sikh religion, and help support the education of Sikhs in the Preston area. The trust appears to be in a healthy financial position with grants rising from £16,000 in 1996 to £30,000 by 1998. The correspondent stated that any type of charity is supported anywhere in the world, but there is a particular emphasis on poverty and children.

Application details: in writing to the correspondent.

Trustees: Jaswinder Singh Kholi; Bhupinder Singh Kholi; Amardeep Singh Dhody; Harpreet Singh Chadha.

Correspondent: Mr J S Kholi, 12 Sherborne Street, Manchester M3 1ED. Tel: 0161 834 8818.

Hans Raj Jain Foundation

Grant total: Not known
Work: General
Beneficial area: UK
Charity Commission number: 1013837

At present there is virtually no information publicly available on file at the Charity Commission, other than that it was established in 1992, with objects described simply as both general and national. However, the foundation is believed to be a grant-maker. Unfortunately, no further information was provided by the correspondent.

Trustees: Tej Paul Jain; Saroj Jain; Tarun Jain.
Correspondent: Mr T P Jain, 51 Lodge Road, Walsall, West Midlands WS5 3LA.

The Hindu Charitable Trust

Grant total: £1,000 (1997)
Work: Hinduism
Beneficial area: Leeds and surrounding areas
Charity Commission number: 258281

The trust, which was set up in 1968 by members of the Hindu community in Leeds, administers the city's Hindu temple as well as running a community centre. However, some very small grants are made in response to clear need amongst the local community. Unfortunately, no further information was available from the correspondent other than confirmation of the trust's grant-making role.

Trustees: Not available.
Correspondent: Mr S C Shah, Chair, 113 Alwoodley Lane, Alwoodley, Leeds LS17 7PN. Tel: 0113 245 3885.

The Hinduja Foundation

Grant total: £104,000 (1995)
Work: General
Beneficial area: UK and overseas (particularly India)
Charity Commission number: 802756

Parmanand Deepchand Hinduja first set up a charitable trust in 1944 following the commercial success of his import-and-export business, based in India but working throughout the Persian Gulf. Along with the beliefs of the Hindu religion, and what he witnessed during and after the partition of India and Pakistan in 1947, he publicly adopted the motto of Mahatma Gandhi: 'A man's true wealth hereafter is the good he has done to his fellow men'.

Parmanad Hinduja began by gathering resources to establish and fund relief centres, organised settlements, and medical care units. In 1951 he set up his first national hospital in Bombay.

In 1968, to co-ordinate the activities of the various trusts of the Hinduja family which were now up and running, the Hinduja Foundation was established as an umbrella organisation. There are three main foundations – based in the UK, USA and India – working principally in the areas of: public health; education; social welfare; sport and culture. Over $100 million has now been donated by the foundations worldwide, although India and its people remain the focus.

The Hinduja Foundation's priorities are:

- to establish and maintain hospitals and provide medical care for the poor and other deserving persons, without reference to religion, caste or creed;
- to establish and support educational institutions, both academic and vocational;
- to encourage excellence through the granting of scholarships, professorships and prizes;
- to provide funds for welfare and charitable purposes;
- to support cultural, religious and social activities;
- to promote sport, and the quest for physical and mental health;
- to provide relief in the event of natural disasters.

The last set of accounts on record at the Charity Commission are for 1995 and show an income of £270,000 for the UK foundation, with charitable expenditure during the year of £105,000. Grants included: £57,000 to the Cambridge Foundation; £5,000 to the India Celebration Fund; £3,000 to the British Red Cross; £2,000 to the Vaswani Lecture and Reception; £1,000 to the NSPCC; and £250 to SANE.

In 1997, the foundation hoped to raise significant funding from the National Lottery's Millennium Commission in a £100 million project called 'Concordia', a multi-faith centre billed by the foundation as: 'a place where adults and children can learn more about the world around them, a place they can realise that, in the ways that really matter, other people are just like them, whatever their language and whatever the colour of their skin'. The foundation aimed to raise partnership funding from the UK Asian business community. Unfortunately the Millennium Commission decided not to support the project. Since then the Hinduja Foundation was linked to a bail out of the 'Spirit Zone' of the much maligned Millennium Dome in Greenwich, but this gesture also foundered. Despite these setbacks the Hinduja brothers are Britain's richest Asians and are said to be worth approximately £1.3 billion, from which the foundation is clearly a direct beneficiary.

Trustees: S P Hinduja; G P Hinduja; P P Hinduja.

Correspondent: Mr David Broad, Vice President, 11 Studland Street, London W6 0JS. Tel: 0171 889 4661 (020 7889 4661).

The Human Relief Foundation

Grant total: £207,000 (1996)
Work: General
Beneficial area: Somalia, Iraq, Bosnia, North Africa, Bangladesh and the Lebanon
Charity Commission number: 1043676

Though only established in 1995, this Muslim-oriented foundation has already comfortably consolidated its financial position, both in terms of what it donates and its asset base, which now stands at £150,000.

The foundation's main geographical areas of interest are Somalia, Iraq, Bosnia, North Africa, Bangladesh and the Lebanon, although it is not limited specifically to these in its objectives.

The principal beneficiary of the foundation's support during 1996 was Human Appeal International which received £129,000. Recipients of more modest awards included the Kashmir Yanteen Trust and Muslim Hands, which both received £2,000.

Trustees: Not available.
Correspondent: Dr Nabeel S Al-Ramadhani, Chair, PO Box 194, Bradford, West Yorkshire BD7 1YW. Tel: 01274 392727.

Humanity First

Grant total: Not known
Work: Relief of poverty and sickness
Beneficial area: UK and overseas
Charity Commission number: 1050934

Humanity First is an initiative of the Ahmadiyya Muslim Association UK and was set up to channel the financial fruits of the Association's humanitarian and charitable activities. From a modest beginning, this effort is now carried out by a registered charity. The Association also has thousands of members in over 160 countries, including businessmen, professionals, students and housewives, providing moral and material support to the under-privileged, the sick and the needy, both Muslim and non-Muslim.

Unfortunately, the information contained on file at the Charity Commission carries limited information on the trust's financial history, grant policy and beneficiaries. The trust's objects are listed as: 'The relief of poverty and sickness amongst people suffering as a result of natural disasters or human conflict, but not exclusively'.

Information provided by the trust detailed its work in both the UK and internationally. In Britain, grants are regularly made to national and local charities including the Royal Marsden Hospital, Mencap, the Royal Hospital for Sick Children in Glasgow, and Oxfam. As part of the worldwide Ahmadiyya Movement the trust supports relief work to victims of armed conflicts as well as cyclones and earthquakes, including working in Bosnia, Somalia, Rwanda,

Sierra Leone, Mauritius, Bangladesh and Japan.

The bulk of the trust's income comes directly from the Ahmadiyya Muslim Association. Although an accurate grant total was not available, the trust is thought to make numerous small grants.

Trustees: Aftab Khan; Mansoor Shah; Nisar Butt; Amatul Ahmad; Ahmad Syed; Mohammad Javaid.

Correspondent: Nisar Ahmed Butt, Treasurer, 10 Hardwick Way, London SW18 4AJ. Tel: 0181 870 4282 (020 8870 4282).

Imam Hussein Foundation

Grant total: Not known
Work: Advancement of Islam; education; relief of the sick, poor and elderly
Beneficial area: UK and overseas
Charity Commission number: 1041856

The foundation was set up in 1994, which is perhaps why there is only basic information currently available on public file at the Charity Commission.

The foundation's objects are described in the trust deed as: 'Islam; advancement of faith and education, relief of sick, poor and aged, in the UK and elsewhere'. The director of the trust is currently based overseas and consequently the foundation is not particularly active. In the past grants have been made to refugee groups across the world. The correspondent indicates that on the director's return, the foundation will resume its grant-making activities.

Trustees: Dr Sayed Tabatabai: A R Peer Mohammed; Mohammad Tawfik Allawi; Ali Muhsin.

Correspondent: M Allawi, 67 St Dunstans Avenue, London W3 6QH. Tel: 0181 992 2904 (020 8992 2904).

Indersen Jasodadevi Charitable Trust

Grant total: £3,000 (1995)
Work: Medical and educational aid
Beneficial area: India and other developing countries
Charity Commission number: 1041757

Created in 1994, this trust has essentially been set up for the benefit of Giwalior, near Delhi in India, though its remit is considerably wider, allowing for support to 'Third World countries'.

The trust's objects are listed as the provision of medical aid and treatment, and the promotion of research and education for poor and needy people, as well as the provision of literacy and educational support.

The trust's size and age mean it has so far made only two notable grants, paying for a portable X-Ray machine, and a portable defibrillator for a hospital in India in grants totalling just £3,000. Its assets in 1995 were believed to stand at around £20,000.

The correspondent states that more recently, although the amount disbursed has not increased significantly, support has been spread to include 'eye camps', family planning projects and support for people with physical handicaps.

Trustees: Dr A P Singhal; Dr Y K Gupta; Dr Parag Singhal; Mrs Poonam Singhal; Dr K Singhal.

Correspondent: Dr K Singhal, 30 Beechwood Grove, Pencoed, Bridgend, South Wales CF35 6SU. Tel: 07990 573960.

India Development Group (UK) Ltd

Grant total: £50,000 (1997)
Work: Poverty, education and training in appropriate technology
Beneficial area: India
Charity Commission number: 291167

Presided over by Labour MP Keith Vaz, this organisation was set up in 1970 by a number of Indian professionals living in the UK who were concerned by the levels of poverty in India, particularly in rural areas.

The group initiates and gives support to community development projects, and forestry and primary health schemes. It helped establish an Appropriate Technology Development Association in India to develop low-cost technology suitable for revitalising village economies, and introducing it to village communities. Since 1989, the group has also established a training institute in Lucknow, Northern India. The Institute trains rural poor youths in skills to enable them to generate income for themselves and their families by the use of small rural technologies. The Institute also gives training in primary healthcare and special forestry to improve the quality of rural life in order to slow the drift to urban slum areas.

Recent grants have been made under the category headings of Women and Rural Development (£24,000), Rural Development and Training (£20,000), and Health and Waste (£3,000).

The resources of the organisation have remained relatively stable over the past 10 years, although according to the last set of accounts available (1996), there was both a fall in income, from £92,000 to under £28,000, and a corresponding fall in the grant total for the year, from £80,000 to £11,000. However this figure rose again to £50,000 by 1997. The correspondent states that since 1996 the trust has secured funds from the European Commission, although no figure is mentioned.

Directors: Raju Abraham; Paul Bishnoi; Kapoor Chandaria; Graham Chapman; Richard Gupwell; Geeta A Meneses; Andrew Redpath; Diana Schumacher.

Correspondent: Surur Hoda, 68 Downlands Road, Purley, Surrey CR8 4JF. Tel: 0181 668 3161 (020 8668 3161).

India Development Trust

Grant total: £2,000 (1996)
Work: Development in India
Beneficial area: India
Charity Commission number: 1041673

This trust is a relatively new organisation, established in 1994, and therefore there is only very limited information on public file. The Charity Commission does have the accounts for 1996, which detail an income of £40,000 and a grant total of just £2,000.

However the trust is clearly well connected and could be expected to become a significant grant-maker in the future. Aside from its distinguished list of trustees, its patrons are the Rt Hon Lord Weatherill, the Earl of Shannon and H E Dr L N Singhvi, the India High Commissioner.

The administrator states that the trust supports 'development-oriented, innovative, problem-solving, sustainable projects benefiting poor and marginalised people in India'. Unfortunately they did not reveal more detailed information concerning who the beneficiaries were and the type of work done.

Trustees: Dr Prem Sharma; Ram Gidoomal; Howard Flight MP; Dr G P Cowley; Mr R Mehrotra; Miss L Dubash; Mr A Popat CBE; Dr S Wirz.

Correspondent: Paul East, Administrator, PO Box 43, Sutton, Surrey SM2 5WL. Tel: 0181 770 9717 (020 8770 9717); Fax: 0181 770 9747 (020 8770 9747); e-mail: 100126.3641@compuserve.com

Inlaks Foundation (UK)

Grant total: £220,000 (1996)
Work: Education
Beneficial area: UK
Charity Commission number: 285595

Set up in 1982 by the late husband of Lakshmi Shivdasani who is notable for being the UK's richest Asian woman, said to be worth £100 million, the foundation's grant levels have remained fairly consistent, leading to an average grants total of over £200,000.

The accounts at the Charity Commission for 1996 show assets of £350,000, with grants listed as: Scholarships (£223,000); Projects (£3,500); and Donations (£100).

In response to a request for further information about the foundation's work, the correspondent simply requested that the entry be removed from this listing. However it is known that the UK-based foundation channels funding from the main Liechtenstein-registered Inlaks Foundation.

Trustees: Count Nicco Sella Di Monteluce; Bina Shivdasani-Sella Di Monteluce; Azad Shivdasani.

Correspondent: Mrs Anita Rahchand, Honorary Secretary, 88 Gloucester Terrace, London W2 3HH. Tel: 0171 724 6906 (020 7724 6906).

International Network for the Development of India in Action

Grant total: £110,000 (1998)
Work: Relief of poverty and education
Beneficial area: UK and India
Charity Commission number: 1051095

The trust was only established in 1995 but has quickly become a relatively large player in the trust world. In receipt of grants from the Overseas Development Administration and other major aid agencies, the trust channels support to a variety of education projects both in the UK and India. The trust is keen to support local issue work, including funding projects in India's tribal communities, as well as educational grants for factory workers. Unfortunately, a list of beneficiaries was not available on public file at the Charity Commission.

Trustees: Not available.
Correspondent: Bhagwandas Badhan, Director, 118 Lordswood Road, Hardborne, Birmingham B17 9BU. Tel: 0121 554 5854.

Islamic Relief Agency

Grant total: £140,000 (1998)
Work: Relief of poverty and education
Beneficial area: UK and particularly overseas
Charity Commission number: 294263

This trust was set up in 1986 for 'The relief of poverty and sickness and the advancement of education'. Detailed information provided by the trust shows that the vast majority of its grants are directed towards overseas relief work, via the Islamic Relief Agency's field offices in Bangladesh, Afghanistan, Sudan, Jordan, Iraq, Pakistan, Bosnia, Mali, Uganda, Chad and most recently Albania. Projects include joint Christian/Muslim-run women's centres in Western Bosnia, support for Kosovan refugees, rehabilitation schemes in post-war areas and assisting returning refugees. The trust is also involved in several multi-faith projects and is in receipt of grant funding from organisations across the world, UK funders including the DFID, the Methodist Development and Relief Fund, and Christian Aid.

The vast majority of the trust's income is raised from the public. A local advisory committee made up of the various communities in the West Midlands co-ordinates fundraising activities.

Only around 5 per cent of the trust's grants are disbursed within the UK and the trust does not normally publicise this information in case it creates too great a demand. Grants tend to be one-off and for no more than £100 and typically are given to refugees who need help settling in the UK.

Trustees: Dr Abdalla Suliman Elawad, Director; Dr Usman Abdelwahab; Dr Ali Elhag Mohamed; Mr Abdalla Hassan Ahmed; Capt Elnur Abdalla Zarroug; Dr El Amin Mohamed Osman; Mr Ahmed Osman Makki.

Correspondent: Mr D Summers, PO Box 1301, Camp Hill, Birmingham B11 1QP. Tel: 0121 766 8771. e-mail: Ukisra@aol.com

Vikram Jadeja Charitable Trust

Grant total: Not available
Work: Art, music, theatre and general
Beneficial area: UK and overseas
Charity Commission number: 1023933

Set up in 1993 to support general charitable purposes, including sponsorships, there is unfortunately a limited amount of information currently available on public file. However, information provided by the correspondent reveals the range of the trust's support. Although grant totals are still not available, grants have been made in support of numerous cultural functions including an 'India Evening' at the Foreign and Commonwealth Office in London, the private view of the 'Padshanama' Mughal Manuscript at the Queen's Gallery at Buckingham Palace, and the Festival of Indian Independence Anniversary in 1997. Other grants include art scholarships to the Jaipur Art College in India, support of mobile eye clinics in India, art publications and numerous grants to large-scale appeals, including Save the Children and Comic Relief.

Trustees: Vikram Jadeja; Sir Richard FitzHerbert; Sajjan Chudasama; Krishna Jadeja.

Correspondent: Mr V Jadeja, Arnold Hill and Co, Craven House, 16 Northumberland Avenue, London WC2N 5AP. Tel: 0171 930 9841 (020 7930 9841).

Jaswant Rai Jain Foundation

Grant total: £0 (1991) but see below
Work: General
Beneficial area: UK and India
Charity Commission number: 328460

Established in 1989, the last set of accounts on file at the Charity Commission show an income of £11,000 in 1991. Although no actual cash grants were made during the year, the trust was involved in the collection of second-hand clothes in the UK and their distribution in India.

Trustees: Mr Rakesh Jain; Mrs Usha Jain; Mrs Reena Tayal.

Correspondent: R Jain, 17 Luttrel Road, Sutton Coldfield, West Midlands B74 2SP.

Johnson & Mukherjee Brothers Charitable Trust

Grant total: £7,000 per annum
Work: Education and leisure facilities for young people
Beneficial area: Yorkshire
Charity Commission number: 1001216

This trust has assets of almost £40,000 situated in a number of endowment funds and disburses approximately £7,000 a year in grants. Information provided by the correspondent gave extensive detail of the trust's work, which primarily involves grant-making to education and leisure projects targeting young people between the ages of 3 and 11 years. The trust will only consider supporting projects run by state schools and will not fund items considered the responsibility of the local authority, or any capital development.

Recent initiatives have included developing science projects in primary schools and numerous other extra-curricular activities. The trust runs closely in parallel with its partner organisation, the Mukherjee Brothers Charitable Trust (*see below*).

The correspondent states that as the trust prefers to work on a small scale no unsolicited appeals will be considered.

Trustees: Joan Johnson; Sib Mukherjee; Nrisingha Mukherjee; Lloyds Bank plc.

Correspondent: Mrs J I Johnson, Secretary, 9 Waldby Garth Road, Keyingham, Near Hull, North Humberside HU12 9TN. Tel: 01964 623940.

The Kafletha Anjuman-E Islamic Trust

Grant total: £8,000 (1999)
Work: Muslims
Beneficial area: Worldwide
Charity Commission number: 328653

Although this trust was registered with the Charity Commission relatively recently, it has been running on an informal basis since 1968. It was started when individuals originally from the Kafletha area of India started sending money back to Kafletha and other villages, to fund mainly educational work. In recent years the trust has significantly expanded its remit and is now involved in supporting a range of Islamic and secular projects. A small number of grants are available to mosques and, in the area of education, funding is available for Islamic degree students to pay the salaries of teachers of Islam, as well as for secular education. The trust also provides support to refugees across the world.

Despite the trust's clear commitment to its work it is reliant on funds from members of the local community and the projected expenditure for 1999 is set to exceed income. Assets stand at around £65,000 and in 1998 grants totalled just £1,200, whilst grant totals in 1997 and 1996 were £2,900 and £2,200 respectively.

Trustees: Not available.

Correspondent: Zainul Abedin Patel, Secretary, 31 Everard Court, Garrett Street, Nuneaton, Warwickshire CV11 4QB. Tel: 01203 329150 (024 76329150).

Kalsi Foundation

Grant total: £2,000 (1993)
Work: Eye clinics
Beneficial area: India
Charity Commission number: 1014627

Set up in 1991 to relieve poverty, sickness and distress amongst people resident in Randhawa, Punjab, India, the foundation concentrates its support on the provision of eye clinics.

In its first year the foundation had an income of £9,000 and a grant total of £2,300 which was donated in its entirety to Dr Kalsi, the Memorial Free Clinic, Punjab, India. Unfortunately there is no further information on public record. However, information provided by the correspondent reveals that the foundation opened a clinic in November 1991 called the Dr S K Kalsi Memorial Free Clinic in Randhawa. It provides general medical services free of charge. After two successful 'Eye Camps', it now has a regular fortnightly eye clinic providing up to 70 consultations a day. Additional information from the correspondent reveals that the founder of the trust, Harjinder Singh Kalsi, who set up the foundation in memory of his late wife, also donates money to an unnamed medical trust which funds four researchers each year.

Trustees: Harjinder Singh Kalsi; Gurdev Singh Ghattaura; Avtar Singh Kalsi.
Correspondent: H S Kalsi, 67 Rose Valley, Brentwood, Essex CM14 4HJ. Tel: 01277 224752.

Kejriwal Foundation

Grant total: £18,000 (1996)
Work: Education and medical
Beneficial area: India and UK
Charity Commission number: 1041639

Established in 1994 by the Kejriwal family, the foundation makes numerous small grants. However, the Anndana Trust in Tirupatti, India, has received the bulk of the foundation's support, including a past grant of £30,000.

The foundation, which is funded solely by the Kejriwal family, makes numerous small grants to education and medical projects both in India and in the UK, as well as to some more general causes. The correspondent states that grants are made as and when there are available funds and that the main focus for the trust's work is on education.

Trustees: Sohan Kejriwal; Robin Meadowcroft; Mukesh Kejriwal; Graham McEneaney.
Correspondent: Mr S L Kejriwal, New Park Estate, Kenninghall Road, London N18 2PE. Tel: 0181 887 0055 (020 8887 0055).

Dr Susil Kumar and Jamila Mitra Charitable Trust (UK)

Grant total: £15,000 (1998)
Work: Alternative medicine
Beneficial area: UK
Charity Commission number: 1006469

The trust was set up in 1991 to 'promote, develop and aid alternative medicine'. The 1996 accounts show an asset base of £425,000, and also, in line with previous years, a grant total of £10,000. Unfortunately, the recipients are not listed in the information on file at the Charity Commission, although, according to the correspondent, they consist of various homeopathic medical charities and include both hospitals and universities.

Grants are awarded bi-annually and the trust advertises before each grant round in a medical homeopathic journal.

Trustees: P Badham; V Vadheera; J Dawson; P Fisher.
Correspondent: P F D Badham, Solicitor, 19 Pitt Street, Kensington, London W8 4NX. Tel: 0171 937 4876 (020 7937 4876).

Mahavir Trust

Grant total: £20,000–£22,000 per annum
Work: General
Beneficial area: UK and overseas, particularly India
Charity Commission number: 298551

Established in 1987, the trust had an asset base of over £120,000 in 1994, most of which appears to have been accumulated over the previous three years, during which period it also made grants of around £20,000 per annum. Unfortunately there were no more up-to-date accounts on public file at the Charity Commission.

In 1994 the trust made grants to a wide range of UK and India-based organisations, ranging from £4,000 to the Navanat Vanik Association UK to £50 to both VSO and Bolton Village. Other beneficiaries included the Institute of Jainology (£1,500), Concern India Foundation (£1,300), Jain Samaj Europe (£1,000), the Samaritans (£100) and Oak Hill School (£100).

The correspondent states that the trustees try to look at most incoming requests, although the focus is on community affairs in the UK and India, disaster relief overseas and in the UK, animal welfare and supporting families.

Trustees: H S Mehta; P S Mehta; J S Mehta; K S Mehta.
Correspondent: Nemish Mehta, 7 Brompton Road, Kinsbury, London NW9 9BX. Tel: 0181 204 4204 (020 8204 4204).

V H Mehta Charitable Trust

Grant total: £1,000 (1991)
Work: General
Beneficial area: UK and overseas
Charity Commission number: 327620

Set up in 1987, this is a small trust with assets in 1991 (the most recent set of accounts on file at the Charity Commission) of just £5,000. In that year income was under £1,000, and grants made during the year included: £50 to the Orchard Vale Trust, £50 to Shropshire Health Authority and £240 to the Royal Commonwealth Society for the Blind.

Trustees: Jayenda Patel; Chotalal Mehta; Bhupatrai Mehta.
Correspondent: Mr V H Mehta, 1 Cherry Orchard Close, Bramhall, Cheshire SK7 3PW. Tel: 01706 898100.

Mercury Phoenix Trust

Grant total: £893,000 (1996)
Work: AIDS research
Beneficial area: UK
Charity Commission number: 1013768

There is very little information concerning this large trust currently on public file, despite assets of over £2.2 million and a high profile background. The trust was founded following the death of Zoroastrian Freddie Mercury, lead singer of the rock group Queen, who died of AIDS in 1990. A large portion of his estate was used to set up the Mercury Phoenix Trust. Unsurprisingly, two of the trustees are Brian May and Roger Taylor, fellow members of the band.

Despite its size, the information available at the Charity Commission is cursory. However, grants are made towards the care, treatment and welfare of people suffering from AIDS. The 1996 accounts show an income of £625,000, slightly down on the previous year, although over the same period the grant total almost doubled to a substantial £893,000.

Trustees: Henry Beach; Brian May; Roger Taylor; M Austin.
Correspondent: Peter Chant, The Mill, Mill Lane, Cookham, Berkshire SL6 9QJ. Tel: 01628 527874.

Idara Minhaj-ul-Quran UK

Grant total: £10,000 approximately (1998)
Work: Recreational facilities for young and elderly people; the advancement of Islamic religion
Beneficial area: UK
Charity Commission number: 1027979

The objects of this organisation are described as general, though it includes specifically: 'the advancement of the Islamic religion and provision of recreational facilities for the young and elderly'.

Though a relatively young organisation, it appears to be growing steadily, with incoming donations to the charity itself reaching £147,000 in 1995 – the last set of accounts on record at the Charity Commission. This raised the trust's asset level to a substantial £300,000. However, grants made by the trust are much more modest, and in the same period donations totalled just £3,000. However, by 1998 it appears that donations had risen steadily, the correspondent stating a total of £10,000. Grants are primarily for assisting Muslim refugees in a variety of locations including Kashmir, Bosnia and Kosovo, as well as providing language teaching.

Trustees: Sufi Mohammad Aslam; Haji Mohammad Younis; Mohammad Afzal.

Correspondent: Haji Mohammad Younis, 292-296 Romford Road, Forest Gate, London E7 9HD. Tel: 0181 257 1786 (020 8257 1786).

Mukherjee Brothers Charitable Trust

Grant total: £10,000 (1998)
Work: Education and leisure facilities for young people
Beneficial area: Lincolnshire, UK
Charity Commission number: 702424

A partner of the Johnson and Mukherjee Brothers Charitable Trust (*see above*), this trust shares trustees and general grant-making priorities, namely the support of extra-curricular leisure and education facilities for young people.

Support is given to local Lincolnshire-based education projects, where it is not replacing or supplementing public or state funding, and funds facilities for the recreation and leisure activities of young people. This amounted to £10,000 in 1998, up from previous years when grants have been made to the Legbourne Map (£2,000) and Legbourne School of Music (£300). Sib Mukherjee has worked all his life in Lincolnshire and established the trust as a way of paying back what he considered he had been given.

As with its partner organisation, unsolicited applications are not currently invited.

Trustees: Sib Mukherjee; Nrisingha Mukherjee; Joan Johnson; Mike Thompson; Professor L Marsh; Mrs E Baker; Norman Riches; Professor Arthur Ridings; John Bushell.

Correspondent: Mrs J I Johnson, Secretary, 9 Waldby Garth Road, Keyingham, Near Hull, North Humberside HU12 9TN. Tel: 01964 623940.

Muslim Aid

Grant total: £1,909,889 (1998)
Work: General
Beneficial area: UK and overseas (primarily Bosnia, Albania and Bangladesh)

Charity Commission number: 295224

Muslim Aid was set up in 1985 as a way of channelling the charitable obligations of two million Muslims in Britain towards people in need overseas. Its founder was Yusaf Islam (former pop star Cat Stevens), who has recently stepped aside from the trust after 15 years to pursue different charitable work. Muslim Aid responds to disasters – sending food, medicine, clothes, tents and numerous other essential items. It also initiates and funds long-term development projects concerned with food, water, healthcare, basic education and skills training. It works with small community-based Muslim and non-Muslim organisations, and has branches in Leicester, Cardiff and Sheffield.

It has a steady income of around £2 million per annum and a similar level of assets. Most of the income is received through donations and bequests, and the recipients of grants during 1995 (the last year for which this breakdown was available) by location include: Bosnia (£366,000); UK (£180,000); Bangladesh (£145,000); and Albania (£93,000). In 1998 it is known that grants totalling £99,000 were made in the UK.

Trustees: Iqbal Sacranie, Chair; Dr Suhaib Hassan, Vice Chair; and 18 other trustees.

Correspondent: Mr Mohammed, Director, PO Box 3, 2 Digswell Street, London N7 8LR. Tel: 0171 609 4425 (020 7609 4425).

Muslim Families Charitable Trust

Grant total: Not known
Work: Help to Muslim charities
Beneficial area: UK
Charity Commission number: 289592

This trust was established in 1984, and the most recent accounts on file at the Charity Commission are unfortunately for 1987. These show an income of £33,000 and assets of £18,000, with no charitable grants recorded up to this date. Objects are simply listed as the provision of assistance to Muslim charities. Sadly the correspondent declined to reveal further information, resulting in a very limited picture of the trust's activity.

Trustees: Ali Abdullah Mughram Al-Ghamdi; Hashim Medhi; Al-Sayed Al-Darsh; Yaqub Zaki; Khali Siddiqi; Hammayun Khan.

Correspondent: Dr Majid Katme, 55 Balfour Road, London N5 2HD.

Muslim Hands

Grant total: £254,000 (1995)
Work: Development and education work
Beneficial area: Overseas
Charity Commission number: 1029742

This trust was set up in 1993 to provide general charitable support and to advance the Islamic faith. The trust appears to work on the basis of giving away as much as it earns each year, leaving an asset level of only £4,000. However, this policy works to the beneficiaries' benefit, as the trust's grants total regularly exceeds £200,000. Grants are made to organisations specialising in long-term development work, especially the digging of wells and the establishment of schools and dispensaries.

In 1995, grants awarded were classified as follows: Kashmir (£65,000); Bosnia (£40,000); Pakistan (£25,000); Education (£13,000). Unfortunately no detail on the actual recipients themselves was available.

Trustees: Syed Hassanain; Newaz Ahmed; Dr Zahid Nawaz; Iqbal Qureshi; Khalil Minhas; Aftab Parwaz; Dr Musharaf Hussain.

Correspondent: S L Hassanain, 205 Radford Road, Hyson Green, Nottingham NG7 5GT. Tel: 0115 911 7222.

The Noon Foundation

Grant total: Not available
Work: Education, poverty, racial harmony
Beneficial area: UK
Charity Commission number: 1053654

Set up in 1996 by G K Noon MBE, founder of Noon Products and a former UK Asian Businessman of the Year, there is very little information currently available on this relatively young foundation. It was set up to support organisations working in a range of areas, including the advancement of education, relief of poverty, promotion of racial harmony, and treatment of the sick and infirm.

Following Noon's recent sale of his company, Noon Foods, for which he received a package worth £50 million, it looks likely that this well-known philanthropist might be able to dedicate both the time and money to advancing the activities of his foundation further.

Trustees: Gulam Noon; Akbar Singh; Zeenat Harnal; Zarmin Sekhon; Sehangir Mehta.

Correspondent: J J Mehta, Mehta and Tengra, 4 Wellington Terrace, Bayswater Road, London W2 4LW. Tel: 0171 242 1942 (020 7242 1942).

Viquaran Nisa Noon & Firoz Khan Noon Educational Foundation

Grant total: £15,000 (1996)
Work: Education
Beneficial area: UK and Pakistan
Charity Commission number: 1017002

This foundation, which was established in 1993 by Lady Noon, specifically aims its funds at the provision of bursaries and scholarships to Pakistanis wishing to study in the UK.

Most of its 1996 asset base of £265,000 was accumulated between 1993 and 1995, and appears to have subsequently fallen off. Between 1993 and 1996 grants totalled £20,000. Unfortunately there is no further information on file at the Charity Commission as to where the grants were made.

Trustees: John Baron; Dr Humayon Khan; John Emly; Sir Nicholas Barrington; Manzoor Hayat Noon.

Correspondent: Mr J M Baron, 39 Newhall Street, Birmingham B3 3DY. Tel: 0121 236 4477.

Parivar Trust

Grant total: £8,000 (1996)
Work: Young people and women
Beneficial area: India
Charity Commission number: 1032529

Set up in 1994 for the benefit of young people and women, in 1996 the trust's assets reached nearly £500,000. However, despite this impressive financial base, grants totalled less than £8,000. Unfortunately there is very little additional information on this trust on public file at the Charity Commission.

Following a request for further information, the correspondent requested that the entry be removed from this listing, stating that: 'this trust does make grants to organisations in India, but all our work is through local contacts there whom our trustees have met on visits to India'. It therefore seems unlikely that unsolicited applications will be considered.

Trustees: Pramila Ramani; Robert Oakley; Nigel Rogers.
Correspondent: Mr N Rogers, 62 Symphony Court, Birmingham B16 8AF.

Ambika Paul Foundation

Grant total: £28,000 (1997)
Work: Education (organisations only)
Beneficial area: UK
Charity Commission number: 276127

Named after his young daughter, who died of leukaemia in 1968, the foundation was set up by steel baron and Labour peer Lord Paul in 1978. The foundation has grown steadily, accumulating assets of £800,000 by 1995. In the same year it raised its grants total quite dramatically to a similar figure of £798,000, compared to £246,000 the previous financial year. However, this does not reflect the true size of the trust's giving as it coincided with Lord Paul's headline-making grant of £1 million to London Zoo. Consequently the grant total of £28,000 in 1997 is said by the correspondent to be much more in line with the trust's true giving potential which is completely reliant on donations from the Paul family.

The trust has no clear-cut grant policy, with grants currently distributed both to universities and community groups. Support is strongest in areas where Lord Paul's Caparo group has an interest. Within that there is also a particular interest in supporting children's projects.

The correspondent strongly requested that charities did not apply to the foundation for funds, stating that as there are no dedicated staff it has 'become an immense burden' servicing the trust. Despite this note of caution, Lord Paul's steel business continues to service the trust, providing administrative support to the trustees who meet four times a year.

Trustees: Lord Paul; Mrs A Paul; Mrs A Punn.

Correspondent: Lord Paul of Marylebone, Caparo House, 103 Baker Street, London W1M 2LN. Tel: 0171 486 1417 (020 7486 1417).

The Pukaar Foundation

Work: Health and welfare, education and training
Grant total: approximately £18,000 (1997/98)
Beneficial area: West Yorkshire, with a preference for the Bradford district
Charity Commission number: 1056702

An initiative of a group of Asian businessmen, the correspondent claims the Pukaar Foundation: 'is the only charitable trust in the UK which specialises in attracting funds from the Asian community, in particular the Asian business community. The trust supports individuals and organisations working towards the improvement of educational achievement, youth unemployment, poor health, homelessness, the arts, community development, business start-up for young people, social exclusion and isolation'.

The foundation was established in 1996 by a regeneration agency called QED which is based in Bradford. The group is a very successful training and consultancy organisation for Asian small businesses. Asian businessmen and businesswomen are asked to contribute to the Pukaar Foundation which is intended to support the whole community. The foundation is aiming to build up an endowment, the investment of which will provide income for projects run by inner city communities, irrespective of their background.

The trust supports registered charities and non-registered constituted groups, and in particular addresses the following issues:

- relief of financial need by providing goods and services;
- costs of training, to assist people in earning a living;
- provision of advice services and other assistance to people who are suffering financial hardship;
- relief of sickness;
- advancement of education, including the promotion of education and training and the provision of scholarships, bursaries and exhibitions.

Grants have ranged from £250 to £2,000 and in 1997/98 totalled around £18,000. The following grants were made in February 1999: £1,000 each to Asian Disability Awareness in Bradford, Asian Women's and Girl's Centre and

West Bowling Youth Initiative, £960 to the Caleb Project and £500 to Key House Project.

Application details: In writing to the correspondent.

Trustees: Mussadik Hussain; Dr Mohammed Ali; Timothy Harvey Ratcliffe; Miss Adeeba Malik, Nisdr Raja; Nazir Hussain.

Correspondent: Zulficar Ahmed, Projects Development Officer, QED Bradford, West Bowling Centre, Clipstone Street, Bradford, West Yorkshire BD5 8EA. Tel: 01274 735551.

The Puri Foundation

Grant total: £56,000 (1996)
Work: General
Beneficial area: Nottinghamshire and India
Charity Commission number: 327854

Established in 1988, this trust had assets of virtually £2 million by 1996. This is largely due to generated income of £70,000, although this amounted to only half the income for 1995. Unfortunately there is no further information on funding policy or beneficiaries available from the records on file at the Charity Commission. However founder Nat Puri features in *Eastern Eye*'s Asian Rich List and is worth £85 million according to their calculations. It is also known that the foundation supports employees and ex-employees of Puri's company Melton Medes, as well as providing equipment to schools, recreation and leisure facilities, and supporting training programmes for young unemployed people in Nottinghamshire. The foundation has in recent years made a funding commitment of £250,000 to the building of a new Hindu temple and community centre in Nottingham.

Trustees: Anil Puri; James Philpotts; U Puri; A R Puri.
Correspondent: N R Puri, Environment House, 6 Union Road, Nottingham NG3 1FH. Tel: 0115 958 2277.

Shri Radhe Foundation

(also known as the Devshi J Chandegra & Radha Chandegra Seva Trust)
Grant total: £7,000 (1996)
Work: General
Beneficial Area: UK and overseas (particularly India)
Charity Commission number: 1039725

Set up in July 1994 by Nanji Devshi Chandegra, this small trust is able to support a range of charitable causes worldwide. It is clearly early days in the trust's development, as assets in 1996 stood at just £1,000, but income in the last two years has totalled almost £20,000.

Grants in 1995 amounted to over £11,000 and were all made to projects in India, whilst in 1996 grants of just £1,000 were made to UK organisations, including SSPCUK, as well as grants to organisations in India totalling over £6,000.

Trustees: Lalitkumar Chandegra; Ramesh Chandegra; Kishor Chandegra.
Correspondent: Mr L D Chandegra, 30 Tranmere Road, Twickenham, Middlesex TW2 7JB. Tel: 0181 563 1740 (020 8563 1740).

Rambapa Sadhu Seva Trust

Grant total: £3,000 (1994)
Work: General
Beneficial area: UK and overseas
Charity Commission number: 1007853
This trust was established in 1992 to advance religion and education, relieve poverty, sickness and suffering, and provide food and shelter. Recently the trust appears to have been relatively inactive, and in 1996 grants plummeted, from £3,000 in 1995 to zero. However, its assets remained at £140,000. Unfortunately there are no further details available as to why this might have occurred.
Trustees: Shri Maganlal Bhimjiyani; Shri Anilkumar Bhimjiyani; Shri Bipinchandra Kantaria; Shri Bhagwan Mirchandani; Shri Lachmandas Pagrani; Shri Lilaram Kewlani; Shri Mukeshbhai Patel; Shri Subhashbhai Chudasama; Shri Jivatram Chandiramani; Shri Ashwinkumar Bhimjiyani; Shri Ramchand Rajwani.
Correspondent: Mrs B J Kantaria, Mercury House, 1 Heather Park Drive, Wembley, Middlesex HA0 1SX. Tel: 0181 903 1919 (020 8903 1919); Fax: 0181 903 1912 (020 8903 1912).

Z V M Rangoonwala Foundation

Grant total: £10,000 (1996)
Work: General
Beneficial area: UK and overseas
Charity Commission number: 271513
The assets of this foundation have remained stable (around £80,000) for some time, as has its charitable expenditure. During 1995 the foundation made grants of £6,000, which in the following year rose moderately to £9,000. Over this same year there was a notable increase in income from £6,000 to £48,000.

Established in 1976, the foundation's objects are clearly broad, and beneficiaries have included: British Red Cross (£1,000); Keynsham Social Group (£1,000); Southwark Youth Project (£500); Airth Scout Group (£250).
Trustees: R J Angus; E Fane Saunders; A Rangoonwala; Miss Jean D'Cruz; K Rangoonwala.
Correspondent: Miss Jean D'Cruz, Honorary Secretary; 123 George Street, London W1H 5TB. Tel: 0171 724 0720 (020 7724 0720).

Rao Fazal Ali Trust (Rao Foundation)

Grant total: £1,000 per annum
Work: Education, poverty, sickness, distress and permanent disability
Beneficial area: Pakistan
Charity Commission number: 1042776

According to its file at the Charity Commission the trust, which is also known as the Rao Foundation, was set up in 1994 to 'advance education and relieve persons who are in need by reason of poverty, sickness and distress'. Activity by the trust seems limited, with its assets standing at present at £15,000.

The settlor trustee, Mr A H Kunwar, informs us that he will commit £1,000 a year for grants and since 1995 over £3,000 has been distributed in grants in Pakistan. Unfortunately there is no published information available on precisely where the money is being allocated although from the correspondent it is known that grants are made to students in need in Pakistan, particularly those for whom economic circumstances or a disability make it impossible to study.

Trustees: Mr A H Kunwar; Mrs H B Kunwar; Mr M J Kunwar; Mr M S Rao; Mr F A Kunwar.
Correspondent: Mr A H Kunwar, 56 Weald Lane, Harrow Weald, Harrow, Middlesex HA3 5EX. Tel: 0181 863 5919 (020 8863 5919).

Sri Satya Sai (UK) Trust

Grant total: £302,000 (1996)
Work: General
Beneficial area: UK and overseas
Charity Commission number: 278481

Established in 1989, the trust's principle grants tend to be made to the Sri Satya Sai Central Trust. In 1996 the Sri Satya Sai Central Trust received an extremely substantial donation of £290,000.

Unfortunately the other beneficiaries, which received grants amounting to £12,000, are not listed. The trust's income for the same period stood at £340,000, leaving an asset total of £90,000. For a trust of this size it is a shame that there is very little additional information available as to the trust's principle aims and grants policy. It is probably worth noting that the financial figures listed above are double that of the previous year.

Trustees: Mr Balram Puri, Chair; Mr C Nathwani; Mr Thadani; Mr H Mansbridge; Mr Kundra.
Correspondent: Mr A Bhagani, Station House, 11 Masons Avenue, Harrow, Middlesex HA3 5AH. Tel: 0181 861 2000 (020 8861 2000).

Sarwar Jehan Charitable Foundation

Grant total: £8,000 (1998)
Work: Islam and education
Beneficial area: UK, Pakistan and Kashmir
Charity Commission number: 327789

This foundation was set up by Professor Ahmad in 1988 in memory of his mother after whom the foundation is named. The Ahmad family are heavily involved in the foundation's work and also provide its financial base. Assets stand at approximately £150,000 and in 1998 grants totalled £8,000. Despite broad objects of the advancement of the Islamic religion, education and the relief of poverty, the foundation appears to focus on the provision of educational scholarships. Support is given to poor students in the UK, Pakistan and Kashmir in both primary and secondary education. This is done through providing part scholarships to the educational institution which then pay for fees and maintenance costs.

Trustees: Professor Khurshid Ahmad; Haris Nazir Ahmad; Asma Khurshid Ahmad; Dr Manazir Ahsan.
Correspondent: Professor Khurshid Ahmad, Chair, 1 Croft Drive, Wigston, Leicester LE18 1HD. Tel: 0116 288 6422.

Shah Bhagwanji Kachra Foundation

Grant total: £25,000 (1997)
Work: Poverty, sickness, education and religion
Beneficial area: UK and overseas
Charity Commission number: 1004398

This foundation was set up in 1991 with a wide remit, allowing it to make grants in support of the relief of poverty and sickness and the advancement of education and religion.

In its first year of operation the trust had an income of £40,000 and made grants totalling what has since proved to be an all-time high of £25,000. Since 1994, grants peaked at £9,000 in 1996/97, when incoming donations totalled just £14,000.

There is unfortunately no further information available on the nature of the grants, or the names of beneficiaries.

Trustees: Somchand Bhagwanji Shah; Bhimji Shah.
Correspondent: B B Shah, 17 Woodgate Crescent, Northwood, Middlesex HA6 3RB. Tel: 0181 566 7100 (020 8566 7100).

Devraj Pethraj Shah Family Charitable Trust
(Jinendra Foundation)
Grant total: £190,000 (1992–1998)
Work: Medical, Jain religion and general
Beneficial area: UK and overseas (primarily South Asia)

87

Charity Commission number: 1014254

Set up in 1992 for general charitable purposes, the trust's main focus is: 'To relieve poverty of students, advance the Jain religion, and to relieve the need of cancer sufferers'.

Most of the grants, which totalled at least £190,000 in the first six years of the trust existence, are made to overseas-based organisations, especially in South Asia, and with a clear emphasis on organisations involved with eye related work. Beneficiaries included: the National Association for the Blind (Bombay) (£2,900); the Rotary Eye Institute (£2,800); Indian Red Cross (£1,500); the Samaritan Eye Hospital (£200); the Jankalyan Charitable Trust (£100). However, the correspondent states that grants are also awarded to other medically oriented causes, including TB and cancer charities. A small number of grants are also made in the UK to a range of causes including hospices, hospitals and cancer charities, as well as overseas development agencies including Oxfam.

Trustees: Jayantilal Devraj Shah; Dinesh Jayantilal Shah; Rohit Jayantilal Shah.

Correspondent: J D Shah, 1 Courtleet Road, Cheylesmore, Coventry CV3 5GS. Tel: 01203 501547/413142 (024 76501547/413142).

K N Shah Trust

Grant total: £1,000 (1994)
Work: Poverty, religion and education
Beneficial area: UK and overseas
Charity Commission number: 289601

This small trust was set up in 1984 to support poverty, religious and educational charities. In 1994 the trust's assets stood at just £10,000, and it had a negligible income of just £200. However grants made during the same year totalled £600 and beneficiaries included Help the Aged, British Red Cross and the Jyoti Eye Hospital, which each received £50.

Trustees: Khetshi Shah; Vipool Shah; Chandrakant Shah.

Correspondent: Mr V K N Shah, 7 Mount Stewart Avenue, Kenton, Harrow, Middlesex HA3 0JR. Tel: 0181 907 0084 (020 8907 0084).

Dr N K Shah Trust

Grant total: £7,000 (1995)
Work: Education and religion (primarily Jainism)
Beneficial area: UK and overseas
Charity Commission number: 327291

Established to support educational and religious projects, the trust has a regular income of around £20,000 per annum. This has aided the creation of a strong asset base, which in 1995 stood at nearly £250,000.

Grants in 1995 totalled nearly £7,000 and beneficiaries included: the Jain

Academy (£1,500); Charity in India (£1,000); Jain Samaj Europe (£250).
Trustees: Bhanumati Shah; Samir Shah; Leena Shah.
Correspondent: Dr N K Shah, 20 James Close, Woodlands, London NW11
9QX. Tel: 0181 455 5573 (020 8455 5573).

Baba Deep Singh Ji Shahid Charitable Society

Grant total: £3,000 (1996)
Work: Poverty, sickness and education
Beneficial area: UK and overseas (primarily India)
Charity Commission number: 1044987
This small trust was set up in 1995 and lists its surprisingly wide-ranging
objects as: 'the relief of poverty; assistance for the elderly, the handicapped and
the disabled; education; marriage guidance; assistance to widows, orphans and
single parents. Provision of Ayurvedic medicine. Relief of the inhabitants of
India'.

From its income of £4,000 in 1996, the trust made grants totalling £3,000
and recipients included the West Bromwich Afro-Caribbean Centre and the
Society of St Vincent de Paul. Assets in 1996 stood at just £1,000.
Trustees: Not available.
Correspondent: Mr J S Birdi, Accountant, 33 Helmsdale Road, Lillington,
Leamington Spa, Warwickshire CV1 2ES. Tel: 01203 220208 (024 76220208).

Tilda Foundation

Grant total: £38,000 (1997/98)
Work: Asian charities, health, general
Beneficial area: UK and overseas
Charity Commission number: 1011933
As the name suggests, the foundation is derived from the Tilda Rice food
company and although currently small is one of the few grant-making trusts
established by the UK Asian business community.

In 1997/98, the trust had an income of £134,000, comprised mainly of
donations. Grants to 20 organisations totalled £38,000. The large surplus, of
£96,000, was transferred into the capital account, resulting in assets at the year
end totalling £131,000. Larger grants were £10,000 to both Raghuvanshi
Charitable Trust and Self Realisation Fellowship, £4,000 to Arpana Charity,
£3,300 to Aim High Appeal, £3,000 to Vasravi Water Works, £2,500 to
Bharatiya Vidya Bhavan, £2,000 to British Heart Foundation and £1,000 to
Childline. Remaining grants ranged from £30 to £500, including £500 to
NSPCC, £250 to both HOPE and Mencap, £200 to Scope and £100 to the
Asian Foundation for Health.

If the foundation continues its intimate relationship with the Tilda Rice
company, income looks set to rise, as Tilda now have over 50 per cent of the
rice market in the UK.
Trustees: S Thakrar, Chair; R Thakrar; V Thakrar; R Samani.

Correspondent: Mr Shilen Thakrar, c/o Tilda Ltd, Coldharbour Lane, Rainham, Essex RM13 9YQ. Tel: 01708 521133

Uwais Foundation

Grant total: £2,000 (1995)
Work: Islam
Beneficial area: Tyne and Wear, UK
Charity Commission number: 1014410
This is a small foundation, set up in 1992 for the purposes of promoting Islam, advancing education in Islamic history and culture, and supporting young people through the provision of social welfare and leisure activities.

Income has remained at around £2,000 per year, with a similar annual grant total. However, although it is known that support is given to projects based in the Tyne and Wear area, it is not known which organisations have received support.
Trustees: M Mushtaq Ahmed; K Najeeb.
Correspondent: Mr Khursheed Najeeb, 113–115 Fenham Hall Drive, Newcastle upon Tyne, Tyne and Wear NE4 9XB.

Charles Wallace Bangladesh Trust★

Grant total: £9,500 (1996/97)
Work: Educational grants to individuals
Beneficial area: UK and Bangladesh
Charity Commission number: 283339
Trustees: P F Fowler CMG, Chair; K Ahsan; P Docherty.
Correspondent: Mr D M Waterhouse, 54 Grand Avenue, London N10 3BP. Tel: 0181 444 8230 (020 8444 8230).

Charles Wallace Burma Trust★

Grant total: £8,000 (1996/97)
Work: Educational grants to individuals
Beneficial area: UK and Burma
Charity Commission number: 289004
Trustees: Lady Susan Fenn, Chair; U Hla Pe Than; P Docherty.
Correspondent: Mr D M Waterhouse, 54 Grand Avenue, London N10 3BP. Tel: 0181 444 8230 (020 8444 8230).

Charles Wallace India Trust★

Grant total: £242,000 (1996/97)
Work: Educational grants to individuals
Beneficial area: UK and India
Charity Commission number: 283338

Trustees: Sir David Orr, Chair; R E Cavaliero; Prof Judith Brown.
Correspondent: Dr Frank Taylor, Administrator, 9 Shaftesbury Road, Richmond, Surrey TW9 2TD. Tel: 0181 940 9295 (020 8940 9295).

Charles Wallace Pakistan Trust*

Grant total: £55,000 (1996/97)
Work: Educational grants to individuals
Beneficial area: UK and Pakistan
Charity Commission number: 283337
Trustees: Sir Oliver Forster, Chair; Prof F R Allchin; Mrs S Hamid; P Docherty.
Correspondent: Mr D M Waterhouse, 54 Grand Avenue, London N10 3BP. Tel: 0181 444 8230 (020 8444 8230).

*Background to the Charles Wallace Trusts

Charles Wallace, a British businessman in India who died in 1916, left his estate to be divided, after provision for his children, between the British Treasury and the Treasury of British India. In his will he wrote that 'all possessions great and small being acquired from or through the people as mine should return to the people'. Trusts were set up in Britain, from 1981 onwards, for each of the four countries of former British India to assist nationals, normally resident in their respective countries, to obtain education or training in Britain. Support is normally given at postgraduate or professional levels (often in the arts or humanities) and can include visiting fellowships, research grants, study awards for students already in Britain and support to British institutions providing training facilities for nationals of the countries concerned. The conditions vary slightly for each trust and those wanting more information should consult the appropriate trust correspondent. Initially, all the UK-based trusts were administered by the British Council. Now, although the Council remains a corporate trustee, the administration is carried out separately. The trusts are all separate entities, although they share common features.

World of Islam Festival Trust

Grant total: £12,000 (1995)
Work: Education of public in Muslim and Islamic cultures
Beneficial area: UK and overseas
Charity Commission number: 313799
This relatively old trust was established in 1973 to advance the education of the public in the Islamic and Muslim cultures. Its last set of accounts on file at the Charity Commission are for 1995 and show an income of £150,000 and assets of £180,000. During the year, the trust made grants totalling £12,000. Beneficiaries included: the Islamic Art Foundation (£2,000); Wellcome Institute (£1,500); Medical Aid/Children of Palestine (£750);

Glasgow Muslims Islamic Art Leaflet (£250).

The correspondent was reluctant for the trust to be included in this listing, stating that it is a 'small family trust'.

Trustees: Not available.

Correspondent: Mr A Duncan, Director, 33 Thurloe Place, London SW7 2HQ. Tel: 0171 581 3522 (020 7581 3522).

Zoroastrian Trust Funds of Europe

Grant total: £95,000 (1997)
Work: Education, children and the Zoroastrian faith
Beneficial area: Worldwide
Charity Commission number: 277185

Formerly known as the Incorporated Parsee Association of Europe this organisation was established in 1978 with assets of £137,000. The trust which was set up with the object of advancing the Zoroastrian faith worldwide makes grants through several pooled funds, including the House Purchase fund, the Memorial Fund, the Educational and Charity Fund and the 2nd World Youth Congress Fund. Assets exceed £1 million and totalled £1,195,000 in 1997, which was up from £1,084,000 in 1996. Total grants rose significantly during the same period, from £36,000 in 1996 to £95,000 in 1997. Unfortunately, particularly given the size of this trust's grant distributions, there was no further information on file at the Charity Commission as to where the funds actually go.

Trustees: Mr B Irani; Mr C Sethna; Mr N Avari.

Correspondent: Dorab E Mistry, 88 Compayne Gardens, London NW6 3RU.

Bibliography

*1991 Census:*Volume 2: Chapter 4, 'Ethnicity in the ethnic minority populations of Great Britain', David Owen, Office for National Statistics, 1996

Asian Who's Who, Asian Observer Publications, 1995/96

Ayahs, Lascars and Princes: Indians in Britain, 1700–1947, Rozina Visram, Pluto Press, 1986

Black and Asian Groups, a sectoral review by the London Borough Grants Unit, 1992/93

Black Perspectives in the Voluntary Sector, P Haughton and T Sowa, Thames/LWT Telethon Report, 1993

Black Voluntary Sector Manifesto, 1996

Britain's Richest Asian 100, Eastern Eye, 1997

Britain's Richest Asian 200, Eastern Eye, 1998

Britain's Richest Asian 200, Eastern Eye, 1999

Confederation of Indian Organisations unpublished report, Draft report for the Home Office, 1996, unpublished.

Defining the non-profit sector: a cross-national analysis, Lester M Salamon and Helmut K Anheier, Manchester University Press, 1997

Dimensions of the Voluntary Sector 1997, edited by Cathy Pharoah and Matthew Smerdon, Charities Aid Foundation, 1997–8

Dimensions of the Voluntary Sector 1998, edited by Cathy Pharoah and Matthew Smerdon, Charities Aid Foundation, 1998–9

Directory of Asian Voluntary Organisations, 1994/95, Confederation of Indian Organisations

Ethnicity in the 1991 Census, Ceri Peach, Office for National Statistics, 1996

Fairness in Funding, R Doven and F Ellis, Association of Charitable Foundations Report, 1996

Funding Black Groups, Mark Lattimer, Directory of Social Change, 1992

'Funding equality to build communities – the work of the National Lottery Charities Board', *Dimensions of the Voluntary Sector, 1997,* Mark Lattimer and Danielle Walker, Charities Aid Foundation, 1997

A Guide to the Major Trusts 1997/98, Luke Fitzherbert, Susan Forrester & Julio Grau, Directory of Social Change, 1997

A Guide to the Major Trusts 1999/2000, Luke FitzHerbert, Dominic Addison & Faisel Rahman, Directory of Social Change, 1999

The Jewish Voluntary Sector in the United Kingdom: its role and its future, Margaret Harris, policy paper published by the Institute for Jewish Policy Research, 1997

Joseph Rowntree Foundation Finding No 79, Kiran Radia, JRF, 1996

'Local income overview', *Dimensions of the Voluntary Sector, 1998,* Matthew Smerdon and Cathy Pharoah, Charities Aid Foundation, 1998

The Millionaire Givers, Howard Hurd and Mark Lattimer, Directory of Social
    Change, 1994

The New Scots: Asians in Scotland, B Maan, John Donald, 1992

The Non-profit Sector in India, Michael Norton, Charities Aid Foundation, 1996

Peopling of London, Rozina Visram, Museum of London, 1993

A Quaker Businessman – The Life of Joseph Rowntree, Anne Vernon, Sessions Book
    Trust, York, 1987

Race, racism and local authorities, Sondhi and Salmon, Local Government Policy
    Making, 1992

Sari'n'chips, Ram Gidoomal and Mike Fearon, Monarch Publications, 1993

Sectoral Review of Black and Asian Groups, London Borough Grants Committee, 1992

South Asian Population Report for Great Britain, South Asian Development
    Partnership, 1992

The Sunday Times Richest 1,000, ed. Peter Beresford, 1998

Telling It Like It Is, ed. Nadya Kassam, The Women's Press, 1997

Trust Monitor 22, 'The good, the bad and the ugly', Susan Forrester, Directory of
    Social Change, 1997

'UK Asian Communities: A profitable market for non-profits?', Rob Wells and
    Anjna Raheja, *Journal of Non-profit and Voluntary Sector Marketing Volume 2*

Wolfenden Report

Useful organisations

Association of Charitable Foundations
4 Bloomsbury Square
London WC1A 2RL
Tel: 0171 404 1338 (020 7404 1338)
Fax: 0171 831 3881 (020 7831 3881)
Website: www.acf.org.uk/foundations
E-mail: acf@acf.org.uk

The Factary
The Coach House
2 Upper York Street
Bristol BS2 8QN
Tel: 0117 9240663
Fax: 0117 9446262
E-mail: TheFactary@compuserve.com

Charities Aid Foundation
Kings Hill
West Malling
Kent ME19 4TA
Tel: 01732 530000
Fax: 01732 530001
Website: www.CAFonline.org
E-mail: cafpubs@caf.charitynet.org

Federation of Charity Advice Services
c/o South Yorkshire Funding Advice
    Bureau
47 Wilkinson Street
Sheffield S10 2GB
Tel: 0114 2765460
Fax: 0114 2780730

Confederation of Indian Organisations
    (UK)
5 Westminster Bridge Road
London SE1 7XW
Tel: 0171 928 9889 (020 7928 9889)

Funderfinder Ltd
65 Raglan Road
Leeds LS2 9DZ
Tel: 0113 2433008
Fax: 0113 2432966

The Directory of Social Change
Publications Department
24 Stephenson Way
London NW1 2DP
Tel: 0171 209 5151 (020 7209 5151)
Fax: 0171 209 4130 (020 7209 4130)
Website: www.dsc.org.uk
E-mail: info@dsc.org.uk

Institute of Charity Fundraising
    Managers
5th Floor
Market Towers
1 Nine Elms Lane
London SW8 5WQ
Tel: 0171 627 3436 (020 7627 3436)
Fax: 0171 627 4754 (020 7627 4754)

London Voluntary Service Council
356 Holloway Road
London N7 6PA
Tel: 0171 700 8113 (020 7700 8113)
Fax: 0171 700 8108 (020 7700 8108)

National Council for Voluntary
    Organisations
Regent's Wharf
8 All Saint's Street
London N1 9RL
Tel: 0171 713 6161 (020 7713 6161)
Fax: 0171 713 6300 (020 7713 6300)

Sia – the National Development Agency
    for the Black Voluntary Sector
Winchester House
9 Cranmer Road
London
SW9 6EJ
Tel: 0171 735 9010 (020 7735 9010)

South Asian Development Partnership
14 The Causeway
Sutton
Surrey SM2 5RS
Tel: 0181 661 9198 (020 8661 9198)

UK Fundraising
Fundraising UK Ltd
36 Palestine Grove
London SW19 2QN
Tel: 0181 640 5233 (020 8640 5233)
E-mail: hlake@fundraising.co.uk
Website: http://www.fundraising.co.uk